Sacred Threshold

OTHER BOOKS BY PAULA D'ARCY

When People Grieve /
The Power of Love in the Midst of Pain
(The Crossroad Publishing Company, 2005)

Seeking with All My Heart /
Encountering God's Presence Today
(The Crossroad Publishing Company, 2003)

A New Set of Eyes / Discovering the Hidden God
(The Crossroad Publishing Company, 2002)

Red Fire / A Quest for Awakening
(Inner Ocean Press, 2001)

Gift of the Red Bird / The Story of a Divine Encounter
(The Crossroad Publishing Company, 1996)

Where the Wind Begins /
Stories of Hurting People Who Said Yes to Life
(Harold Shaw / Random House, 1984)

Song for Sarah /
A Mother's Journey through Grief and Beyond
(Harold Shaw / WaterBrook Press, 1979, 2001)

Sacred Threshold

Crossing the Inner Barrier
to a Deeper Love

Paula D'Arcy

A Crossroad Book
The Crossroad Publishing Company
New York

The Crossroad Publishing Company
16 Penn Plaza–481 Eighth Avenue, Suite 1550
New York, NY 10001

The poem by Hafiz on page 71 is "In a Tree House" from *The Subject Tonight Is Love: 60 Wild & Sweet Poems of Hafiz,* translated by Daniel Ladinsky. © 1999, 2003. Reprinted by permission.

Printed in the United States of America on acid-free paper

The text of this book is set in 11/15 Stone Informal. The display face is Present.

Library of Congress Cataloging-in-Publication Data

D'Arcy, Paula, 1947-
  Sacred threshold : crossing the inner barrier to a deeper love / Paula D'Arcy. – [Rev. ed.].
    p. cm.
  ISBN-13: 978-0-8245-2465-4 (alk. paper)
  ISBN-10: 0-8245-2465-9 (alk. paper)
  1. D'Arcy, Paula, 1947- 2. Christian biography–United States. 3. Love–Religious aspects–Christianity. I. Title.

BR1725.D34A3 2007
277.3′082092–dc22
[B]

                                                    2006101718

  2   3   4   5   6   7   8   9   10   14   13   12   11   10   09

Contents

We ask too little of life.... We dream too small.

— John Kirvan, *God Hunger*

Don't Miss
Your Life

In 1984 I published *Where the Wind Begins,* a book that has been out of print for several years. It was a collection of stories about people who encountered life with particular courage, and for many readers this book was a favorite among my titles. Three years ago I tried to edit it for renewed publication, but found that both my life and my theology had moved too far past those early days.

Sacred Threshold, twenty years later, is in some sense written in the spirit of that first collection of stories,...

but these stories are seen through the lens of a continuous narrative whose focus is love, love that exceeds the normal bonds and calls out: Don't miss this. Don't miss your life. There's infinitely more than the experience of love we already know. Push against your borders. Dare to move through the next threshold to the freedom awaiting you.

The individuals in these stories all affected me deeply, and I am grateful for their generosity in allowing me to recount our shared experiences. Each story is told with the explicit permission of those mentioned, and this willingness is further expression to me of the kind of love toward which this book beckons. In particular, two of the stories came about because of my work as a therapist. The first involves a young boy, now a grown man, whom I met while I was a counselor in training. The second involves a now public figure, Morrie Schwartz, who invited me to share with him a beautiful aspect of his dying.

Particularly in the case of Morrie, even as we moved through the hours we spent together, we were aware that what we experienced might be powerful and helpful to others. "Pass this on when I'm gone," were words Morrie frequently repeated, knowing that I felt, as he did, a keen sense of our common humanity, as well as a responsibility to give back to this world by helping others discover all that is possible in their lives. Even so, I never had a sense of urgency. Morrie knew that I *would* pass it on when the moment was right, when the right book unfolded, as this one has, dealing with the very nature of love's power that was speaking to us so directly almost ten years ago. On a personal level, the "right" time has demanded that I too stand before a critical threshold, just as Morrie did.

———————— ❦ ————————

THERE'S INFINITELY MORE THAN THE EXPERIENCE OF LOVE WE ALREADY KNOW. PUSH AGAINST YOUR BORDERS. DARE TO MOVE THROUGH THE NEXT THRESHOLD TO THE FREEDOM AWAITING YOU.

———————— ❦ ————————

The very nature of my relationship with Morrie, which created the rich experience I tell here, was a well-considered exception to the usual rules, as the story will reveal. Indeed, in the course of my many years as a therapist, Morrie was a single exception. Even so, it is important for me to emphasize that the story being told did not occur within the confines of therapy. Therapeutic hours remain, as they must, inviolate and confidential. I reveal only what Morrie expressly asked me to share: the power of our first meeting (since first meetings often shape everything that will follow) and the poignant series of encounters that occurred when two human beings looked together, intensely, at the mystery of both death and life.

A New
Vista

The CD spinning on my stereo is *Hidden Music*, a gift presented to a hundred or so donors following a fundraising event that featured the gifted and remarkable conductor/singer/songwriter/musician, Craig Hella Johnson. The melody and lyrics of the lead song are haunting. Over and over Johnson intones that we are all part of the human heart. After the song ends I say out loud, *I am part of the human heart.* The image speaks to things that are foremost in my awareness today: the seeming singularity of our many lives, yet, truly, the oneness of humankind; the realization that there is a fullness waiting to emerge in us, a hidden grandeur in the depths of the atom, the stars; the truth that the immortal *is* our substance. And this immortal brilliance presses within us to awaken our sleeping souls, *for the sake of this world, for the sake of the human heart—a heart ultimately capable of more than it yet imagines.*

Questions have lived in me since I was young: *How much am I willing to know? Will I unsettle my life in order to grow? Do I really want to know where the power of love can take me? Can I leave home, over and over again (figuratively, and perhaps literally) in order to know what is true?*

WHAT IF WE GLIMPSED AND ACTUALIZED THE POWER THAT LIES WITHIN US AND YIELDED TO ITS FORCE? BECAME ITS CHANNEL? BECAME COMMITTED TO GRASPING OTHER HANDS IN OURS AND REACHING TOGETHER TOWARD EVERYTHING WE ALREADY ARE?

Throughout history exceptional men and women have made daring choices in order to ensure freedom from oppression and to correct societal ills. But what would change for this world if a critical mass of men and women began to reach for a truer love and a greater freedom *primarily for the sake of the human heart, for the evolution of humankind?* What if we approached our life span in a greater way? What if we glimpsed and actualized the power that lies within us and yielded to its force? Became its channel? Became committed to grasping other hands in ours and reaching together toward everything we already are?

Who will show us the way? Who will teach us to endure and to prevail? Who will help us find the veiled mystery, the hidden brilliance in our midst? How will we find eyes to see the Spirit in matter? Johnson ends his CD suggesting that perhaps we are angels for one another. *If only we will be.*

Beginnings

In 1989 I made a three-day and three-night vision quest, fasting not only from food, but also from companionship, reading...from every usual distraction. Alone in nature, I eventually began feasting on the only thing that was there: the natural world. Creation. Nature became my food, and suddenly I was communicating with the environment in a way I hadn't thought possible. I became conscious of the ebbs and flow of the river, the unfolding of leaves, the opening of flowers. The language of birds and trees revealed itself. I thought about how often I've heard life described as a feast. I now knew that to be true, but not from an intellectual knowledge. I knew it from the experience of being *with* something, and being willing to let it speak to me from within.

When my quest ended it was clear to me that Eden is not a fanciful, exquisite garden from a former time or for a future dream. The *Earth* is Eden, but hidden by veils of ignorance that keep us from seeing this truth that is right in front of our eyes. *Gift of the Red Bird* was my attempt to put that awakening into words and hold it out to others. Yet in the years that followed I was deeply sobered by another awareness: I saw the extent to which our plentiful and "advanced" Western culture surrounds us with distractions that make the already difficult task of looking at life from an inner place even more difficult. Millions of us spend most of our non-working hours in front of television screens, computer screens, and hand-held screens of every description, never guessing how this impacts our spirit. There is no way to calculate the weakening effect this assault of stimulation has on the human soul and heart. The same amount of hours spent in a forest, watching the oceans and rivers, or studying the web of a spider would be exponentially life-changing. But our imaginations do not tell us that. We cannot see it.

Several years after completing my vision quest I returned to the desert to support six individuals who were taking that same step. I went along to help maintain the base camp and to offer love and support. (Three of the questors were personal friends.) Walking away from civilization in such a determined and intentional way is a challenging threshold. For those of us who were not raised close to the earth, there are many fears for safety and a great sense of unknowing. We all spent the first day setting up camp and putting up a tipi large enough to give shelter and provide space for a camp kitchen. A Native American friend was in charge of the trip and the camp, and he showed us what needed to be done. The full responsibility of the trip and everyone's safety was his, so I took my agreement to assist him very seriously. On the second morning he and I watched as the five men and one woman making the quest left the security of our enclosure and walked off into the desert to spend their three solo days and nights in nature. They carried water, a sleeping bag, and a tarp.

It was surprisingly emotional for me as I watched each of them walk into the distance. *I want to go too.* The feeling rose up inside of me with force, unexpected. With imagination I followed them, knowing that they would go their separate ways somewhere along the trail. They would find their own private circle of earth well away from anyone or anything and begin to look within for guidance. I knew the power of that. I knew how much learning was possible when you confronted yourself in the silence of the desert with nothing to distract you from your deeper nature. Why hadn't I decided to make the quest too? Why hadn't that occurred to me? Why did I arrange the days away and travel to the desert, but limit myself to doing routine chores in a base camp? My disappointment in myself was keen that first morning. I spent the day exploring my new habitat, taking in the smells and sounds. By evening I'd finally settled in. I let the regret go and fully gave myself over to the experience.

WHEN MY QUEST ENDED IT WAS CLEAR TO ME THAT EDEN IS NOT A FANCIFUL, EXQUISITE GARDEN FROM A FORMER TIME OR FOR A FUTURE DREAM. THE EARTH IS EDEN.

Telling the story today, over a decade later, I laugh. Just because I was not "formally" on a vision quest, I convinced myself that the time did not hold the same potential for me as it did for those making the quest. *I'm only the supporting cast. I don't have the lead in the play.* A foolish conclusion, because Nature makes no such distinctions. She reliably, consistently responds to the heart and spirit turned toward Her in openness and love. For Her, the smaller context of our lives is irrelevant and transitory. I'd forgotten that. Whether or not I was making a vision quest, sweeping up a base camp, or (the worst) trying to maintain calm as a tarantula waltzed through the tipi, I, too, was living in the desert with my normal distractions far removed. I wasn't fasting, but I ate minimally. I slept on the earth, and feasted on the movements of light that covered the Chisos mountains. I spent hours watching cactus buds open toward the dawn or listening to the wind. The stream of chatter that regularly floods through me did not have a willing host. After forty-eight hours of being soothed by the desert light and the surrounding silence, I felt a great peace.

On the third and final evening before the questors returned to camp, I took a long walk at sunset, breathing in this last night of solitude. Covered in dust from head to toe, my clothes heavy with the clay of the soil, my hair a nest of matted snarls, I was a spectacle. And I didn't care. My reflection in a mirror (if I'd had one) never seemed less important. I sat in the dirt by the side of the road for over an hour, my walking stick on the ground beside me. I could feel the difference in how I related to things after spending only four days touching the rocky earth, sleeping with my ear attuned to the rhythmic hum of her energy. The physical closeness had produced an inner serenity and a gentle sense of well-being. Watching the red and purplish orange streaks across the night sky was all the heaven I needed. I waited until only the thinnest brush strokes of light remained before I reluctantly pulled myself to my feet and began the slow walk back to camp in the growing dusk.

─────────── ❦ ───────────

MILLIONS OF US SPEND MOST OF OUR NON-WORKING HOURS IN FRONT OF TELEVISION SCREENS, COMPUTER SCREENS, AND HAND-HELD SCREENS OF EVERY DESCRIPTION, NEVER GUESSING HOW THIS IMPACTS OUR SPIRIT.

─────────── ❦ ───────────

I followed the path for several minutes, walking slowly, lingering occasionally to acknowledge a rubbery desert creature that had darted noiselessly from in between two small bushes, a slippery flash of green. Then suddenly I heard footsteps behind me. Assuming that the camp leader had taken his own walk in the beauty of the evening shadows and was about to catch up with me, I stopped to wait for him. But I didn't turn around to wave or acknowledge him. We were the only two people who *could* be on this path. Instead, I kept looking ahead of me toward the last threads of daylight. His footsteps continued, but after a couple of minutes he still hadn't reached me. I finally turned around to judge his distance from where I was standing. Only then did I realize that my friend was not there at all. But something else was. And nothing in my proper, New England upbringing prepared me for what my eyes recorded.

Behind me, in the haze of twilight, as far as my eye could see, was a long line of women walking slowly along the path that wound through the desert night, circling the mountains. Their faces were obscured, heads bent, each one dressed in a native costume whose colors and styles represented dozens of nations. Their skirts moved softly across the dust and swept over the rocks and small shrubs, the only sound their footsteps. I blinked again and again. But each time I reopened my eyes, the women were still there, walking. I was shaken and unsettled by the vision of them...by seeing a vision at all. I tried to clear my head and resume my walk, glancing over my shoulder every few hundred feet. But each time I glanced back, they were still there, still walking. It was as if they were following me. Yet even though they continued to walk at a measured pace, they never caught up to me. I watched them with my physical eyes, but apparently they were moving in a different dimension.

--- ❦ ---

BEHIND ME, IN THE HAZE OF TWILIGHT, AS FAR AS MY EYE COULD SEE, WAS A LONG LINE OF WOMEN WALKING SLOWLY ALONG THE PATH THAT WOUND THROUGH THE DESERT NIGHT, CIRCLING THE MOUNTAINS.

--- ❦ ---

When I reached the last bend in the road before camp I turned around a final time. The path was now empty. They were gone. Or, at least, they were no longer visible to me. I had no reference point for what I had just experienced. I briefly imagined telling my friends, *Guess what I saw?* But the rest of the conversation would be what? I may as well report a UFO. A lantern light was glowing in the tipi, so I knew our leader was there. I stood pensively outside the opening for a while, then stepped in. He was sitting cross-legged on the ground, and he looked up as I entered. He studied my face. Then he broke into a slow grin. "What have you just seen?" he wanted to know. (He seemed to know from my eyes that I had seen *something*.) I blurted it out. He nodded. Then he asked if I had questioned the women? What did they want? Why had they become visible to me? I felt so foolish. It had never occurred to me to talk to them. Instead, I'd stayed astonished and afraid.

Sleep did not come easily that night. I lay on my sleeping bag watching moonlight move through the opening at the top of the tipi, the place where the fabric stretched to create a circle for the poles. When I closed my eyes, in the shadows of memory, the long line of women appeared. They moved in waves. They moved into my dreams. They left me trying to understand what I'd seen, or even the fact that I'd seen it at all.

The six questors returned to camp the following morning. The leader and I dressed before dawn and stood to the east of the tipi, our eyes searching the distance for signs of movement. The light finally came. Then one by one they all came into view, walking slowly toward camp. We greeted them with great emotion. I found myself stifling tears. They were thirsty, hungry, fatigued. Yet their eyes were brilliantly alive; they had exceeded their usual sense of awareness, and the experience changed their demeanor. Each one took some time to break the fast. They ate the stew we'd prepared and then sat alone to record impressions of their days in a journal. They slept. Late in the afternoon we formed a circle around the ceremonial fire and each person was invited to share one experience from his or her days in solitude. The only woman, my friend Maureen, went first.

She spoke about an experience she'd had at twilight, the evening before. She emphasized that while she had *seen* nothing with her physical eyes, she nevertheless had the strong sense that she was suddenly surrounded by women from all over the world. *That they were filling the desert.* Her impression was strong. I barely looked up as she spoke, increasingly moved by the fact that she'd had an experience so close to my own, *on the same night, and at the same time.* As a member of base camp, I was not expected to speak that evening. But when Maureen finished telling her story our leader asked me to tell her and the others about my own encounter.

So I told the circle what I'd seen. There was nothing, really, to interpret, no meaning that was clear. We had simply had the experience, two of us, of women from all over the world making us aware of their presence. What impacted us, beyond the wonder of the vision, was the fact that we had both received it. Driving home from the desert that evening I had increased respect for the reaches of consciousness that are little known to us. There are such large places yet to know.

Two weeks later, my days in the desert behind me, I began a trip across country with my daughter, Beth. Our plan was to drive from Connecticut to California, letting the road take us wherever it would. But first, while driving through the Midwest, I'd promised Maureen that I would lead a women's retreat she was sponsoring. It was delightful to see her again so soon. We talked a bit about the retreat that would begin the next day, and I went to bed early. But at 3:00 a.m. I awakened suddenly and completely. *The women from the desert vision were again present.* This time I could not see them physically, but they were there. It was a powerful sense of their presence. I sat up, turned on a light, and reached for my journal. Then I asked the question I had failed to ask before. *Why are you making yourselves known to me?* As I experienced impressions I began to write. I wrote without lifting the pen from the paper. When the impressions stopped I turned off the light and went back to sleep.

Maureen was waiting for me when I arrived in the dining room the next morning, glad that I was an early riser. She had something she was anxious to tell me. Well, me too, I said. But you go first. *In the middle of the night,* she said, *I awakened suddenly, certain that the women were present again. I got up and walked outside. Their shadowy forms were there in the mist.* I looked at her, shook my head, and told her of my own evening's experience. Then I took my journal and read the words I had written down. In part, this is what I recorded:

Beginnings

We are the voices of generations of women who have walked the Earth. For centuries we have cooked, nurtured, and created homes. We have loved passionately and borne children.

Our wombs are the vehicle through which truth inhabits human form....

We have also watched generations of women forget who they are....

We've watched women separate from themselves, and from the strength within them.

WHAT ARE YOU WILLING TO OFFER TO THE WORLD? YOU ARE PART OF THE HUMAN HEART. ARE YOU WILLING TO STEP THROUGH A DOORWAY, SIGHT UNSEEN?

We have seen the power of the Feminine weakened....

But we have kept a flame burning.

Even when the light within women has grown dim, still, it has burned.

We are the force of generations of patience: waiting, knowing, praying....

We say to the women of today: See who you are. See with the eyes of your heart.

You have ways of knowing greater than the power of reason. Listen to the Voice within. Make time for it. Honor it.

Tell women to begin to walk with us. Tell them to pay attention to their own perceptions. Tell them to prepare the Earth for [a truer] love.

Tell women it is time. They will know.

In the months that followed I thought often about the words I had recorded. I wasn't sure how to respond to the presence of the women, but I continued to tell close friends about a growing urgency to organize a gathering of women from all over the world, a circle that would exceed race, religious affiliation, politics. Just gather the women. One spirit, one heart. *The human heart.* Women ready to respond to the power within themselves, a power able to effect change in the world and healing for the Earth. But I knew we would have to think differently and imagine boldly in order to bring this circle to life. I talked, but I never took action. Years passed. The dream never died, but predictable obstacles arose in my mind, all of them limitations of vision and imagination. *I knew nothing about large event planning.*

There were no financial resources to fund this. The details would be staggering.

And yet, a second voice: *What are you willing to offer to the world? You are part of the human heart. Are you willing to step through a doorway, sight unseen? Are you willing to respond to the soul that lies deep within, and encourage others to do the same?*

Who will give us courage and strength? Unless it's true that we are, ourselves, the very Mystery that can effect change.

Speaking
Visions
into Life

Erin is in her thirties, vivacious, beautiful, and filled with infectious enthusiasm. We met during a two-year period when I lived in California, and I was immediately drawn to her. Her life is a tangle of wonderful husband, growing children, tending bee hives, raising chickens, writing, producing, creating, and becoming a voice for sustainable living. We spent some wonderful mornings curled up on the sofa at a local coffee shop sipping herbal teas and dreaming. But on this particular morning in February 2005, we were huddled together

on a rock jutting into the Pacific Ocean on the coast-
line of northern California. A strong, cold wind sent
waves thundering against the rock, the resulting spray
creating a cold, lacy shower. I watched the gulls as they
dipped fearlessly close to those gray swells of water,
immune to cold or fear. I wished I were as free.

LET'S TEACH OTHER WOMEN WHAT WE NOW KNOW:
THE POWER IS NOT IN THE STORM. IT'S WITHIN US.
WE CAN CHANGE THE WORLD IF ONLY WE THINK
DIFFERENTLY. THERE'S INFINITELY MORE TO KNOW
ABOUT THE POWER OF LOVE AND WHO AND WHAT
WE TRULY ARE.

We'd been talking about our lives as women, the challenges and the joys. And standing there, braced against
the biting cold, I told Erin my dream about creating a
great gathering of women, and how *someday* I would
drive that dream into reality. Her eyes never left my
face. We were huddled together for warmth, just inches
apart. She looked straight back at me and said, *The
name of the gathering will be WOMENSPEAK.* Yes, I said,
as if we were reading from a rehearsed script. I added,

WOMENSPEAK 2007. March 2007. I paused. *San Antonio.*
Erin nodded. *San Antonio.*

The moment still gives me chills. It was spoken into
being that easily. We never looked back. We invited
eight other women, ages ranging from the twenties
to nearly eighty, and met with them in San Antonio
five months later. We rented a ballroom and workshop
rooms at the San Antonio Convention Center for March
2007. We didn't have a dime, and we signed the con-
tracts anyway. Our imaginations saw something, and
we knew intuitively that all we had to do was step fearlessly into that vision and be the midwives for love and
possibility.

The stories that follow are about living life in just such
a manner. In terms of WOMENSPEAK, I dreamed of gathering women together to help them access their dreams
and respond to their souls. The very creation of that
event caused all of us to enlarge our visions of how we
might live. How could it be otherwise? We watched in
amazement as women stepped forward to be part of the
vision. Hundreds of them. They offered their skills, their
time, their talents, their wisdom, their art. They donated
flowers to fill the convention center ballroom. They gave
their song lyrics and songs. They created websites. They
sent money to pay the bills, to buy materials, and to

register women who don't have ample resources. They rushed at us like waves. They created bookmarks and cards and jewelry and gave all the proceeds to WOMEN-SPEAK. They volunteered to speak without pay. They kept coming, kept walking toward us.

The initial deposit for the Convention Center, nearly $5,000, due in the fall of 2006, was paid entirely by women gathered in Louisiana following the devastation of hurricane Katrina. Some had just lost their homes, their belongings, their clothes. All had felt fright and were exhausted in their reaching out to relatives and neighbors. Yet it was these same women, tears filling their eyes, who handed me a basket of cash, checks, and pledges and said, *Here, let's teach other women what we now know: The power is not in the storm. It's within us. We can change the world if only we think differently. There's infinitely more to know about the power of love and who and what we truly are.*

As I watched them, images began to blur. They were wearing their one remaining garment, the one salvaged from the rising water, but I could also see them in a different form. They were walking on that desert path, years ago, sweeping dust into the soft folds of their long dresses. They were women from Louisiana and Mississippi and they were more than that... they were spirits who inhabit the world, having within them the power to shape life and give it new birth. They were gulls daring to dip close to the swells of the sea, unafraid. They were who we might become.

Attuning
Hearts

Attune your heart to the right thing, a voice whispers from within. *Look past what's occurring on the surface.* My daughter Beth once gave me a collection of sayings from Maya Angelou, and I stand one of them on my desk where I can see it every day. *"Hope and Fear cannot occupy the same space at the same time. Invite one to stay."* I made a choice. I invited hope.

But I've also learned that the willingness to take new risks does not arise spontaneously. The new adventure is the harvest. But long before the harvest, well before renting convention centers and bringing visions to life, well before daring, comes something else. Preceding the boldness are years of plowing, planting, and long, soaking rains.

The stories that follow are the rain. They are the early moments that began drawing me toward hope, not fear. They are the reason future bold steps are possible. They are a slice in time, a season in life when something first challenged me to live and love beyond the bounds. Sometimes I paid attention immediately; just as often I was distracted and preoccupied, and even turned away. But the visions and Love were/are relentless.

FOR A BRIEF PERIOD, THIS HEALING LOVE MOVED WITH PARTICULAR INTENTION THROUGH OUR JOINED CIRCUMSTANCES, CREATING A BRILLIANT CRUCIBLE IN WHICH WE WOULD ALL DECIDE WHETHER OR NOT WE WERE WILLING TO BE CHANGED, WILLING TO LIVE IN A NEW WAY.

This rain began when I was enduring a difficult passage in my life. I had just experienced the painful end of a marriage, and all my inner edges were raw. Beth was in her senior year of high school facing decisions that would set a course for her own life. She and I were living temporarily on the second floor of a two-family home, sharing one car, so I often walked the two miles to a small office where I practiced psychotherapy.

In the fall my walk was a feast of color. Then the damp chill of New England winter set in, making every step an act of courage. That winter there were seventeen snowstorms over a three-month period. Black ice covered the sidewalks in slippery patches. As I pushed my weary body along treacherous streets, I thought grimly that the roads I walked were a perfect mirror of my inner terrain.

That same winter my father suffered multiple strokes and was in the last months of his life. My relationship with him had always held many challenges, and as he weakened, I knew there was little time left to resolve some final things. Then a man named Morrie Schwartz appeared in my life. I had known him for only two or three months when he learned that he had amyotrophic lateral sclerosis (ALS), a neurological illness that suddenly pointed him, without regard for his dreams, toward the end of his life. Aware of the imminence of death, Morrie surprised and challenged me with a request that, if I agreed, would define a period of eighteen months in both our lives.

At this same time I also began volunteering as a counselor on Sunday afternoons in a nearby women's prison.

I hadn't expected the experience to mean so much, but Julia, one of the inmates with whom I met regularly, was beginning to affect me deeply. In the prison, in my hours with Morrie, in the regular visits I began to make with my father, and in the difficult aftermath of a broken marriage, I grew increasingly aware of a purposeful force of healing and love laboring to emerge in all our lives. Something was fighting to be known; something seemingly longed to direct each of us to new meaning and sight. And for a brief period, this healing love moved with particular intention through our joined circumstances, creating a brilliant crucible in which we would all decide whether or not we were willing to be changed, willing to live in a new way...willing to wrestle until the full power of Love awakened us to new fullness, engaging not only our imaginations, but the human heart.

Listening
to the
Power
Within

The most dramatic, far-reaching decisions often begin in quiet moments. It was a Saturday morning in April 1993, and at 10:00 a.m. I was still lying in bed, a thick green comforter wrapped tightly around me, pulled so high it even covered my head. My eyes looked, unseeing, through the small opening I had created for air. The room was still. There is something that enables a person to rise each morning, ready to face the details of the day ahead, but on this particular morning, the magic of that life force was no longer mine. A single thought presented itself to me: *A vital part of me is slipping beyond my reach. If I don't change my life, I will lose myself altogether.*

In some way I knew that I'd already let things go too far. I was swimming far from shore.

As I struggled to focus my eyes on the small square of sky visible through the bedside window, a stream of sunlight found its way through the windowpane and moved in ribbons across the wicker headboard. *How had I allowed myself to fall into such a small place?*

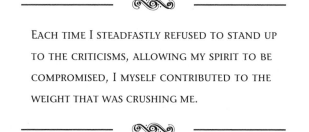

EACH TIME I STEADFASTLY REFUSED TO STAND UP TO THE CRITICISMS, ALLOWING MY SPIRIT TO BE COMPROMISED, I MYSELF CONTRIBUTED TO THE WEIGHT THAT WAS CRUSHING ME.

I watched myself as I lay there and saw a woman who had become a stranger to herself. I had been widowed in 1975 (my husband and daughter Sarah were killed in an accident involving a drunk driver) and remarried in 1987. The decision to marry again had been hopeful, but the experience had not played out easily. There were so many factors. I postponed our engagement once because I had reservations. It felt like the decision was too rushed. I was concerned that my fiancé's discomfort around my friends was a hint of strong differences in our natures. But I let myself be convinced that my reservation was unreasonable and only the product of my own fear.

In truth, there *was* substance to my caution, and discounting my own truth was the first herald of the unhealthy dynamic that would follow. My partner's judgments about things very basic to my sense of well-being, such as the way I related to others, my interests and tastes, my appearance...all accelerated as soon as we were married. Every shred of my esteem began to erode, until I was enduring steady, reproachful words without resisting. Each time I steadfastly refused to stand up to the criticisms, allowing my spirit to be compromised, I myself contributed to the weight that was crushing me.

In reality, I was living with verbal, emotional, and mental abuse, but I couldn't have named it at the time. My only experience was a rising fear. I hated what was happening, but seemed paralyzed to make a change. Eventually one of my sisters called, pleading with me to recognize what was happening to me. Apparently, in spite of my efforts to keep my situation well hidden, it was obvious to her and other family members with whom she'd spoken that something was wrong. Part of me knew she was right; another part felt too afraid to act. Fear had me in its grip.

Moving ever so slightly beneath the quilt that day, I knew that something was willing me, then and there, to finally fight the weight that pressed on me from all sides. But where did that impulse come from? I didn't know. It was simply there.

Sunlight now spread across the accordion-pleated lampshade, breaking into streaks of yellow and red as it stretched across the shade. I watched the colors and found myself thinking of a long forgotten story. I remembered a fairy tale told by Clarissa Pinkola Estes in *Women Who Run with the Wolves.* With no preamble, the story was there, willing itself to break through the dense fog that encased my mind like a linen sack, its drawstrings pulled tight. I searched my memory for a title to the tale. "Sealskin/Soulskin?" Yes. I lay in bed and told myself the story.

There was once a woman who wore the skin of a seal. She lived happily in the sea, fully alive in its great abundance. One night, in order to dance with other seal/women atop a great rock in the sea, she slipped off her skin and laid it on the rock. But when it was time to return to the sea, her skin was not there. It had been stolen. She searched and searched, but it was nowhere to be found. For years afterward she lived on land and wept for the fullness she had once known and for the Great Soul with whom she had lived in the sea.

Then one night as she slept, the woman heard someone calling to her from the ocean, over and over again, until at last something in her awakened. She rose from bed and prepared to leave the confines of her home, having heard the sound of her true self, calling. She walked outside as if in a trance, blindly following the sound, and at the edge of the cliff that dropped to the sea, she saw the "skin" she'd lost. Joyously putting it on, she moved toward the roaring waters. The deeper she dove into the water, the more her life force returned, until finally her lost sight was restored. She was no longer separate from herself. Her skin had been found.

Emboldened by the tale, I got out of bed and pulled on the jeans I'd left in a heap on the floor the evening before. Finally naming my experience had brought something to life. Something within me knew the importance of the tale's wisdom, and knew what I had to do. It had been too long since I'd listened to the truth deep within.

❦

I went to the phone and called my mother, who lived an hour away. She was occupied nursing my aging father, his life radically changed by the effects of surgeries for bladder cancer and several strokes. None of her hours were idle, yet I knew there would be health care aides to relieve her. I asked her to meet me in the driveway and let me take her to lunch. I didn't want to go inside and have to wrestle with my conflicting feelings about my father. Not on this day.

My mother stood waiting for me in the driveway, leaning against the garage door. The years had begun to shrink her frame, and she stood hunched slightly at the neck. She was oblivious to appearance these days, too exhausted by the hours of caring for my father. Her soft gray curls were tucked beneath the cotton kerchief she'd knotted beneath her chin in order to protect her ears against the wind, her upper body lost within the folds of a cream-colored car coat. I noticed that one sleeve of her standard navy blue sweater was pulled down past the edge of the coat's right cuff. She wore stockings, as she always did, in any season, and on her feet were the sensible brown laced shoes that gave her arthritis some small relief.

When my car came in sight, she waved to me with a smile and began moving toward the car. I knew that in just an hour she'd walk slowly back inside that house and again pick up the burden of her chores. It was a twenty-four-hour demand that she now shouldered. A demand weighted by the accumulated efforts of fifty years of marriage, during which she had often over-looked her own needs. For this hour, at least, she had a respite from her usual routine.

We found a small local sandwich shop, and as soon as we placed our order I leaned across the table and told my mother that I was leaving my marriage. That's the knowing I'd faced when I'd gotten out of bed two hours earlier. After three years of hard struggle, I was finally admitting to myself that this was what I had to do. I would have advised any other woman to do the same. But living with the effects of someone's rage had significantly weakened my own sense of power. Now everything in me demanded that I move my daughter Beth and myself away.

The decision had risen up from some deep well of knowledge that was trying to guide me, and I could not continue to ignore that inner voice. I had ignored it for too long, and as a result, I was slowly dying. Like the seal/woman, I had lost my skin. I had stopped being true to my deepest self.

I told my mother that I was frightened and didn't know how I'd find enough courage to go on. I'd always been the person on whom others had leaned. Even when I had suffered the crushing loss of my first husband and daughter in my twenties, I tried to help others bear the loss. I raised my surviving daughter by myself for ten years, figuring out how to rebuild my life. When I re-married, Beth was eleven, and it appeared to be the end of heartache and the opening of a bright new chapter. But the dream I was reaching for and the reality I found were very different. I'd made a decision that wasn't right for either of us, and lying to myself about it had taken its toll. No amount of wishing, no effort, had made it right.

THE DECISION HAD RISEN UP FROM SOME DEEP WELL OF KNOWLEDGE THAT WAS TRYING TO GUIDE ME, AND I COULD NOT CONTINUE TO IGNORE THAT INNER VOICE. I HAD IGNORED IT FOR TOO LONG, AND AS A RESULT, I WAS SLOWLY DYING.

My mother timidly asked for a few details. For the last five years I had been careful not to speak of my situation. Even though my mother's intuition had told her that I wasn't happy, she still hadn't guessed the realities of our situation. I hadn't been able to afford to have her or anyone guess what was happening until I could face it myself. Now as I described my circumstances, my mother reached for my hand. "I understand," she said quietly.

Then from somewhere deep within, my mother began to speak. Through all the years, we'd never had such a conversation. The force of her words was palpable. She told me that there was within me all the strength I needed. I couldn't have imagined it at the time, but in that moment she was passing on a wisdom that has been passed on, woman to woman, through all the ages. She was directing me to seek guidance from within. She looked at me. "You were always so strong," she said. "I never saw your vulnerability." She was thoughtful for a moment, almost speaking to herself. "But if you are vulnerable, like me, then perhaps *I* too have strength like yours." Her words reached into me. Then she shifted back to the conversation at hand. "Listen," she said. "You can do this, and you must."

She told me that she wished I had someone wiser with whom to speak. Since I had known the beloved minister Norman Vincent Peale for several years, and had worked for his Center in New York, she asked what I thought he would advise if I could be sitting with him instead. I smiled. It was so like my mother to assume that someone else would have something wiser to say. But I knew his advice would be no different than her own. I told her that he would tell me to look within for strength, just as she had.

"Then you *are* hearing him say it," she said. She squeezed my hand. "You have to find yourself and act." And with those words, my mother pushed my sealskin across the table of a crowded restaurant and pleaded with me to put it on. She summoned everything she is or ever wanted to be, to be present to me in that moment, and she was momentarily radiant. Feeling as if she had very little to offer, she was telling me exactly what I needed to know: *I was too far from home. Even for the noblest reasons, I had stopped listening to my own soul.*

⸻ ❦ ⸻

THAT DAY, I SAW MY MOTHER IN A VERY DIFFERENT LIGHT. SHE MADE IT CLEAR TO ME THAT MY LIFE WOULD STAY THE SAME UNTIL I BECAME UNAFRAID TO LOOK WITHIN FOR ANSWERS, AND THEN TO TRUST THE AUTHORITY OF THAT KNOWLEDGE.

⸻ ❦ ⸻

As she spoke, I realized that she was encouraging me to claim an awareness that was not common to many women of her age. Having played out her own life so differently, within the confines of strict rules and roles, she nevertheless reached forward in one magnificent gesture and helped give birth to freedom in me. I drove home in tears. In willing labor, my mother had twice given me the elements for life. That day, I saw my mother in a very different light. She made it clear to me that my life would stay the same until I became unafraid to look within for answers, and then to trust the authority of that knowledge.

That night I started listing the "lies" I needed to unmask. As I wrote, I considered that many things I'd been told and had accepted did not, in fact, ring true.

LIE: A problem is a catastrophe. "Something's wrong" when difficulties arise.

INNER KNOWLEDGE: A problem is a summons. A problem is a call to re-examine your life, looking well beneath the surface. A problem is uniquely capable of revealing what needs to change. A problem is the stumbling stone on which healing may begin.

LIE: Bitterness just happens. Some people are bitter "by nature."

INNER KNOWLEDGE: Bitterness is a choice. We shape our lives by what we pay attention to. Whether or not I'm happy is up to me.

LIE: You can attain certainty and control.

INNER KNOWLEDGE: You can only attain the illusion of certainty and control. They aren't real. We live with mystery, which demands trust and great fidelity to deeper truths, not to external realities.

LIE: Be productive and your life will have purpose. Find romance and your life will have meaning.

INNER KNOWLEDGE: Purpose and meaning come from God. Demanding them from any other place will become a false pursuit.

LIE: You must obey all the "rules." You must stay within bounds.

INNER KNOWLEDGE: Beyond the rules is another realm, waiting to be known. Beyond the bounds of earthly love is where a greater love begins in earnest.

LIE: Life comes at you, and all you can do is dodge the bullets and try to find a way through.

INNER KNOWLEDGE: You can pull life toward you. You can create. There is within me that which is greater than my circumstances.

❧

Telling the truth to myself was an important place to begin. I got into therapy and began to pay attention to the nuances. I hadn't betrayed myself in large gasps. I lost sight of my inner wisdom by taking too many shallow breaths. Now I was learning to take breaths that were deep.

———————— ❧ ————————

NEVER HAD I BEEN MORE AWARE OF THE HEROISM IT
SOMETIMES TAKES JUST TO GET UP AND FIND YOUR
WAY THROUGH A SINGLE DAY.

———————— ❧ ————————

I left my marriage, grieving for both my husband and myself, and Beth and I moved onto the top floor of a two-family home. I sold several pieces of furniture in order to move out on my own. We were missing some vital tables and chairs, but lawn furniture worked well. It seemed to suit this life in transition. Every step required great effort. I strained my wrist tightening the shelves of a six-foot bookcase that I'd put together on my own, fiercely proud of my accomplishment. Then the bookcase collapsed within an hour of my standing it upright. Some of the books hadn't even left the boxes. With tears, I stacked the shelves and the books on the floor and pressed on. I did all of this while still working full time, immersed in other people's lives. It actually helped. It reminded me that we walk together, all of us.

I sat in my little office and listened with great compassion to those for whom life presently made little sense. Never had I been more aware of the heroism it sometimes takes just to get up and find your way through a single day.

As fall became winter, a biting cold set in. And then the snow. I imagine Siberian winters to be no different. For weeks there was no sunlight. I skidded on ice three times, trying to back into my small garage, losing a side mirror each time. The General Motors dealership knew me on a first-name basis. Eventually I gave in to nature and parked the car in the driveway, resigning myself to clearing snow from my car and my path every morning.

I was also desperately trying to clear my own heart and mind. A decade earlier I'd learned the hard lesson of setting priorities. I not only *believed* in the necessity of creating a life well balanced between work and play, soul and body, I taught it to other women. I talked about heeding guidance from within. My words were even in print. I grimaced inside: *now* look at me. Fine example *I* was. If I were an alcoholic, I would be saying I'd had a relapse. Why was this so hard? I walked the snowy streets of Boston aware that healing hadn't ended ten years ago. It had only begun. I'd shaped up the outline of my life, but there was much more to realize and important changes still to make. Healing has so many layers, and old habits are relentless. The force of one's culture is relentless. But all of that was excuse. I followed the advice I often gave others and got to work.

However well I understood that the roles I play are not who I am—that I am the Self experiencing those roles— this was still, apparently, something I needed to learn at deepening levels. Because if I had been fully aligned with that Self and her knowledge, I would have chosen differently. It was a sobering realization. But instead of turning the awareness into a self-rebuke, I decided to use it to ignite greater learning.

I began with questions. *Which activities in my life were taking up more time than they were worth? Which relationships nourished me? Which ones didn't? Where should I invest more of my time? How much time did I still spend trying to please everyone? How often was I silent, listening?*

I knew I had choices about whether or not to live in the world differently. But would I actually change? Change didn't require a degree in theology. All the concepts in the world wouldn't benefit me. I needed the discipline required to make the inner journey as primary as I said it was.

I turned a new page in my journal. I wrote, *God is not an idea.* I let those words confront me. *God is a reality. A real Power. And I exist because of that Power, but I have to be willing to know it.* Just a belief in God would not take me far enough. I wanted to live increasingly aware of the hidden force of God.

Then it became clear: The access point I sought was the present moment. If I were always living in my mind, always rushing, always doing, then I would consistently miss the subtle movement of Spirit. I needed the spaces in between my actions to enlarge. I needed pauses. My ear had to be bent to a different ground.

THEN IT BECAME CLEAR: THE ACCESS POINT I SOUGHT WAS THE PRESENT MOMENT. IF I WERE ALWAYS LIVING IN MY MIND, ALWAYS RUSHING, ALWAYS DOING, THEN I WOULD CONSISTENTLY MISS THE SUBTLE MOVEMENT OF SPIRIT.

I created a small checklist: *Guaranteed Ways to Miss the Hidden God.* My subtitle was: *How to Make Mistakes and Miss the Voice Within.*

1. LIVE your life at high speed. No exceptions. Run hard.

2. STAY scattered and distracted. The more clutter and activity, the better.

3. TAKE everything personally. Never evaluate. Agree.

4. USE blame liberally. It's so invigorating. I wasn't responsible; *you* were. Everything's your fault.

5. DON'T laugh, especially at yourself.

6. STAY tied to your past. Elevate it to greatness. Live remembering and longing. Or missing. Why do it halfway? Go for it.

7. USE the word "because." "I can't change, because." Because is so little appreciated as a solvent for responsibility. Try using because. This *will* work.

8. NEVER question or think for yourself. Just keep moving and accepting. (Refer to #1 and #3.)

9. CONTINUE to think of God as invisible and distant. Surely not present in this room. At this moment. Not while I'm reading a book.

10. REINFORCE the belief that your life is going to happen soon. This is *not* it, not yet. But one day. Maybe when I finish reading.

My therapist tried to help me acknowledge the part of me that had always known this marriage was not right for either my husband or myself; *I just didn't listen.* I overrode my own knowledge and intuition, paying more attention to outer voices than the one within. Something was trying to guide me, yet I looked the other way. I didn't take the time to let my reservations speak. I trudged through many feet of snow, contemplating that fact. Knowing that an inner source of guidance was there (and vital to my well-being) was one thing, heeding it was another.

The point was not to draw my own conclusions and then to make thoughtful corrections and adjustments along the way. Listening meant taking a different road at the very beginning. Listening meant changing how I related to everything because it meant changing where I responded *from.* What was driving me? Head? Heart? Soul? Which voice had my greatest attention?

Light dawned slowly. Happiness is never found by appeasing others, nor by trying to keep peace at any cost. People and circumstances are movable. I'd been trying to keep the tide from flowing. *Knowing who you are is what brings happiness.* And gradually, I found my way back home. My outside world continued to buckle, but the peace of reclaiming my skin made everything bearable. I realized that I owed sincere gratitude to this season of heartache. It was difficult to learn at such cost, but without this healing, no future relationship of depth and love would ever have been possible for me, nor any sense of freedom. You can't be free while still hunting either for yourself, or for love. You're free when you

know that you already possess everything you n
lationships are "in addition to" your own worth and
loveableness, not the source of them.

———————— ❧ ————————

KNOWING THAT AN INNER SOURCE OF GUIDANCE
WAS THERE (AND VITAL TO MY WELL-BEING) WAS
ONE THING, HEEDING IT WAS ANOTHER.

———————— ❧ ————————

I prayed that this tumultuous time would be the cause
of equal growth for my former mate. It seemed to me
that some persons come together in order to experience
harmony and pleasure; others, apparently, join in order
to create opportunities for great learning and growth in
each other's lives. I had entered our marriage with so
little understanding. I left knowing the importance of
heeding inner guidance and claiming your own voice.
I also learned that in order to truly love someone else,
you first have to be in possession of your own skin.

Since I'd walked toward the marriage openly, I now
wanted to exit with as much grace. It hadn't gone the
way we'd planned. It didn't match our expectations. It
involved pain, hurt, and struggle. But it had still been
a gift. How else do you describe a crucible in which you
are rescued from false gods and shown so much about

the true nature of love? Ethel Person, the celebrated psychoanalyst, says it well, "Something does not have to end well for it to have been one of the most valuable experiences of a lifetime."

❧

After our first year in the upstairs apartment, the new owners decided to live in our space and asked us to vacate. Beth was almost ready to leave for college, the worst time to make one more transition. A friend stepped into the gap, and we moved into her small rental condominium in Cambridge, which had miraculously become available at just that moment. I gave Beth the single bedroom, and I slept on the couch, knowing that Beth would soon be in a dorm room with even less space.

Then the frustrations began. Whenever I used the stove, the fire alarm was set off by the steam. We lived stepping over boxes. Beth's emotions were on red alert as she prepared to leave home for the first time. It was undoubtedly what Dickens meant when he said, "It was the worst of times." Sometimes at night I would circle for thirty or forty minutes trying to find a place to park on the crowded streets of a busy city. One night I thought I'd have to drive back to my office and sleep there, but a space finally opened. I learned to parallel park with amazing precision, necessity being the mother of at least some dormant skills. Still, I was grateful for this port in the storm.

YOU CAN'T BE FREE WHILE STILL HUNTING EITHER FOR YOURSELF, OR FOR LOVE. YOU'RE FREE WHEN YOU KNOW THAT YOU ALREADY POSSESS EVERYTHING YOU NEED. RELATIONSHIPS ARE "IN ADDITION TO" YOUR OWN WORTH AND LOVEABLENESS, NOT THE SOURCE OF THEM.

And even as the outward struggle raged, healing continued. Inner awareness pressed from within. Questions repeated themselves without ceasing: *What did I really want? How seriously did I mean the things I said about letting Spirit lead the way? I felt like a convict confronted with her prior record. I had a history of abandoning myself. I had done it repeatedly. It would take courage to finally change.*

Discerning whether or not someone else was trustworthy had only been part of my struggle. The greater issue was whether or not I could trust *me.* If I could, then other answers would be clear because I would *know* when I was walking into harm's way. I would know because I *did* know. *I knew because a guiding spirit warned me. But I had to be heeding her. I had to be heeding her most of all.*

I thought of the many places I'd gone for advice and all the mentors I'd consulted. The books I'd read. *A Grieving Time. Getting the Love You Want. We. Grace and Grit. Journey of the Heart.* Every word contributed to my healing, and some of the mentors were invaluable in helping me recognize blind spots and find new perspectives. But all along, *I already knew.*

The force of that awareness overwhelmed me. All the wisdom I needed to navigate my course had always been there.

You Only Bring Yourself

I was their second choice. The chaplain of a nearby women's prison had called to see whether I would provide an evening program for inmates, but she had no idea who I was. She'd wanted my friend, the well-loved author Macrina Wiederkehr, to come and address the women. But Macrina's schedule was full, and she lived over a thousand miles away in Arkansas. She told them I was local and suggested they call me instead.

I went because the prison chaplain begged me, and it seemed heartless to say no to a Sister. One night. I could at least give an hour for a good cause.

In the parking lot, as instructed, I popped the trunk of my car and removed every piece of jewelry, including my watch. I threw in my pocketbook. I removed my car key from a key ring bursting with keys, each one representing entry into the busyness of my life. From my wallet I retrieved my license. It was a strange exercise with a great deal of power.

The message was driven home very clearly: when you walk through those doors, you bring only yourself. Your education and degrees no longer serve you. No one cares. Your level of income is irrelevant. Your pretenses are dangerous. Nothing will get through the metal detectors but who you really are.

Sister met me at the first guard station and escorted me. After passing through several metal doors and the first, twisting courtyard, I had already lost any sense of how to retrace my steps. I was now inside the system.

The meeting room was large, and my eyes took in a single microphone standing in the center of a worn, wooden stage. I tried not to show how scared I felt.

At Sister's suggestion I stood by the doorway in order to greet each inmate as they entered. I waited there while she fussed with the microphone and the arrangement of chairs. Finally a bell sounded, and waves of denim began to move down the corridor. I heard them before I saw them, and I stood there comforting myself with the knowledge that no one was forced to show up for this talk. My audience hadn't been coerced into attending. But I also knew that any special gathering was probably preferable to an hour of work duty or sitting alone in your cell. The fact that they were coming did not mean they really wanted to be there or cared at all about what I had to say. It meant that the alternatives were less appealing. Maybe they were simply starved for a face from the outside.

THE MESSAGE WAS DRIVEN HOME VERY CLEARLY: WHEN YOU WALK THROUGH THOSE DOORS, YOU BRING ONLY YOURSELF.

I was surprised by the friendliness and gratitude I sensed as each woman greeted me. *"Thank you for coming to be with us."* They smiled shyly and shook my hand. Some eyes avoided me, but most looked right into my own. My God, I thought. How does it come to this? No woman plans to end up in prison.

Did any of them have advantages growing up? Good homes? Education? Did they have families, children? Surely they loved and were loved. They longed for things. Were we wildly different, or different at all? I couldn't presume to know anything about their pain ... or even be sure I had anything to say that would matter to them. But one intuition was strong. *If I wasn't going to be real with them, I ought to have stayed home.*

Eighty women filed slowly into the room. Many of their faces were weathered, worn. Their smiles revealed cracked, discolored teeth. Or no teeth at all. Some wore faded headbands that had lost all elasticity. A few women sat alone, but most found seats next to their friends. Once they were seated, the initial spark I'd seen as they welcomed me seemed to fade. Some women now looked sleepy-eyed and distant, most simply lost in pain. Only their bodies appeared to fill the space in front of me; their attention might be hard to win.

I was introduced, and my "credits" never seemed so humiliating. I felt sick and wanted to shrink, praying that Sister would stop speaking about what I had achieved. So what, that I had a master's degree? It didn't prove that I'd learned one thing about life, or that I had ever truly loved anyone. It didn't mean there was any reason for them to respect me. I was listening to the usual litany of my accomplishments with such different ears. Would there be any common ground? We were eighty women sitting in the same room, and that was all, unless my heart could reach theirs.

When I finally stepped to the microphone, all eyes were watching me. I took a deep breath and dove in, doing the only thing that made sense to me. I told them my own story of pain and loss, and what I knew of the hard fight not to be crushed alive by pain.

They listened quietly. For a while I had little sense of what they were thinking, with the exception of one woman with wire-framed glasses and curly blond hair who was sitting in the front row. Her eyes, her body language...everything about her was taking in my words. She was petite and lively, exuding an irrepressible energy. My eyes moved back to her face repeatedly, my only identified ally. But when I offered to answer questions and hear their comments, the whole room came alive. That was when I knew they had been listening. They were hungry. Ravenous. And they wanted to talk. The atmosphere in the room shifted, and I forgot that I was in a prison. I even forgot that I was the second choice and hadn't particularly wanted to come. I was only aware of a circle of women speaking with authenticity and power from their burning hearts.

❦

When the bell rang to send them back to their cells, I didn't want to leave and I didn't want them to go.

Sister led me back through the courtyard and the metal doors, guiding me all the way to the waiting area where I would finally exit. *Please come back,* she pleaded. *Give these women any amount of time that you can. Sit with them one on one.*

I WAS ONLY AWARE OF A CIRCLE OF WOMEN
SPEAKING WITH AUTHENTICITY AND POWER FROM
THEIR BURNING HEARTS.

I couldn't, of course, no matter how my heart tugged at me to do so. My schedule was already full, and my traveling prohibited such a luxury. I wasn't consistently at home. I was a moving target. But Sister either didn't hear me or didn't care about my thin excuses. *Please.* I flashed back to the last part of the evening, when I was distributing the books donated by two of my publishers. The inmates stood around me in clusters, waiting for autographs. The bright, blond-haired woman was there. *Please.*

Sister kept up a good pace, walking beside me and planning the best day for me to return. She apparently didn't hear "I can't." She behaved as if I were accepting her invitation, not refusing it. She moved past my reasons for not returning as if she were water flowing unimpeded to the sea. *Okay, I finally said.* (What else could I say?) *I'll come back just once. I'll return one more time.* She looked at me. *Okay, maybe twice. But that's all I can do.* She finally let that be, and I pushed through the last door and found myself back outside. It was over. I thought I'd peel out of the driveway, but I couldn't even fit my key into the ignition. I laid the key on the dashboard and sat looking through my open window at the moon the women I'd just met could not see from their cell blocks. Another car pulled out of the lot, and the prison froze like a framed picture in the glow of its headlights. And I bent my head onto the steering wheel and wept.

I went back as often as I could. I went when I was too tired to move, jetlagged, weary in my bones. And each time, they breathed new life into me. I sat with them, one by one, in a room too barren and uncared for almost to bear. Even the one scraggly spider plant was struggling for life in its plastic pot. There was an old desk in the room, scratched and chipped, and two wooden chairs with metal legs that I pulled into the middle of the small space in front of the desk. I didn't know why they came. I could fix nothing, I had no answers. I'd have needed a legitimate magic wand and the power to change their past, let alone their present or the future, to bring much hope. But they came so gratefully. *Thank you. Thank you for remembering us. I never thought you'd really come. Thank you.*

I was given permission to give one of the inmates a journal so she could begin to write poetry. She had short, dark brown hair and eyes like a deer that darted continually around the room. Her body was square and strong, tough. She held the journal in her hands and ran her fingers over the cover as if it were sable or mink instead of cardboard.

THE GIVER ALSO KNEW THAT IN A SYSTEM STRIPPED OF COLOR AND SWEETNESS, THE SPIRIT HAD TO BE NOURISHED.

A beautiful young woman, soft, not hardened like so many, showed up one day at someone else's appointed time. Long waves of chestnut hair spilled over her shoulders and fell across her face. She was already sobbing when she walked into the room, and it was a while before she managed to tell me that the baby she'd given birth to in prison six weeks earlier had been taken from her forever that morning. The inmate originally scheduled to see me at this time couldn't bear to witness this young mother's pain. She wanted to help, but had nothing to offer until she remembered that she had an appointment with me. And even though she'd been waiting for three weeks to see me, she gave her appointment away. When the young mother stood at the door after our time together, she looked back and asked, *Do you think this is how the mother of Moses felt when she let him be placed in the basket?*

Their stories and the obvious love among them were having an effect on me. As one woman said, "Outside these walls you can believe that your actions are isolated. Inside these walls you live a different truth: All our lives are interconnected." A fury of anger would spread like fire. But so did compassion. They pulled for one another. They saved one another. Julia, the woman with blond hair who sat so eagerly in the front row that first night, told me that for the first few weeks after her arrival in prison, one of the women kept placing candies and other little unexpected treats for her to find under her pillow. It was an act that, if discovered, would bring reprimand and punishment. But the giver also knew that in a system stripped of color and sweetness, the spirit had to be nourished.

Julia reflected on the gesture, eight years later, and said, "a letter, a visit, a smile, a covert spoonful of ice cream are magnified a thousand fold in meaning. Underneath the layers of mental illness, drug damage, and appalling manners is still the hope that a little love will fall upon them."

꩜

I was stunned by how the inmates kept hope alive for one another, and how potent a force that "little love" was. They did not live "waiting to be released." They lived knowing that "this is it." This day is life. One spring I lived vicariously through the small garden that Julia and her cellmate had been given permission to plant and were tending. First the zucchini and squash were eaten by aphids. The cucumbers survived the aphids only to be eaten by ants. The tomatoes alone remained. In Julia's words, "For weeks we watched, watered, and weeded. She prayed while I removed stems, but the tomatoes remained green. Then one day—in what seemed to be an overnight metamorphosis—an orange-yellow splotch appeared. By nightfall, my cellmate was toting a coveted harvest into our room. Using a plastic knife, she exercised more surgical precision than would ever have been possible with a scalpel. Spreading the mayonnaise on fresh, white bread, she gently placed the juicy slices on top. Our eyes met and held as we simultaneously took our first bite. It was not just the taste of the tomato. It was the harvest...the work in the garden...the miracle of nature...friendship...survival...life...all that in a single, simple bite."

That same year I gave Julia some verses from a poem by the Persian poet Hafiz.

> Light
> Will someday split you open
> Even if your life is now a cage....
> Love will surely bust you wide open
> Into an unfettered blooming new galaxy....
> A life-giving radiance will come....
> O look again within yourself,
> For I know you were once the elegant host
> To all the marvels in creation....
> From a sacred crevice in your body
> A bow rises each night
> And shoots your soul into God....

A month later I sat with Julia, whom I had grown to love, and we faced the fact that she was in prison for drunk driving. There we were, our two chairs drawn together, knees touching, huddled in the godforsaken little room where we always met. A single, dirty pane of glass in the door gave the guards their requisite view of us. The paint on the walls was scraped and discolored; nothing here had been scrubbed or tended with any care. But we were oblivious to our surroundings. We looked into one another's eyes and tried to comprehend the irony of our lives being drawn together at all.

The automobile accident that Julia was involved in resulted in the deaths of a father and child, a loss identical to my own. We talked about the ten seconds that had irrevocably changed both our lives. It made no sense for us to care so deeply about one another. To anyone looking at us from the outside, we would appear to be on opposite sides of a great divide. Then we both began to cry, and neither of us could stop. I threw my white cotton jacket over the arms of our chairs and reached for Julia's hand underneath the cloth, hoping the guards wouldn't notice. I hadn't cried that deeply in years, and only once or twice in front of someone else, ever. But I wasn't crying for me. I was crying for her. We each wept for one another.

⁓◈⁓

Julia described the women in the correctional facility as "broken dolls." It was her first impression of their faces when she arrived. She'd expected those faces to be hard and sadistic. Instead they were "cracked and rumpled, looking with longing for someone to patch them up and hold them a few more times. It is hard to look at these women objectively, once you live with them, hear their stories and share their lives. Despite the crudeness, the essence of humanity in these women is very much alive."

While in prison, Julia completed her bachelor's degree. She also encouraged a number of women to learn to read as well as to earn their GEDs. I eventually learned that many of the women who eagerly accepted the gift of my books on that first night could not read at all. One woman told me that she simply held the book each night. It defied my reason to watch their remarkable battle for hope and meaning. The indignities were endless. Random strip searches. Stripping naked before a guard, every orifice probed. Being allowed fifteen minutes to attend a parent's or child's funeral, having been brought there in waist chains and shackles, regardless of whether or not you posed any threat. Being put into solitary confinement for giving shoes or clothing to a fellow inmate who was cold or suffering. In fact, *knowing* that would be your punishment, and doing it, regardless. "Hearts brought to life by wire and chain," is how Julia described it.

And then the mystery of it all. Some of them were freer than most people I knew. Truly free. Again, Julia's words, written while in prison:

> We're both confined, the sun and I
> Restricted to a time and space
> She watches planets orbit by
> I[watch] humans in their race
> She knows I crave a different place
> Creamy shores of an empty beach
> She marks days with her smiling face
> Brings freedom closer, within [my] reach

Julia taught me that "what is really of importance and value in life is what you have when you are standing naked in a barren room."

She went before a parole board several times, and even though her behavior in prison had been exceptional, each time parole was denied. She accepted the defeats and continued to use her time within the walls to live. It had been a difficult feat to face her crime, an act that was responsible for two deaths and caused irrevocable scars in many lives. Through her pain she confronted what she could not change. Then, even within the walls of a prison, she learned to grow and thrive.

The last time I saw Julia within those prison walls I smuggled in a gift. The risk was great, I knew. I sweated profusely going through the metal detectors, trusting that the search of my materials (I was leading a three-day retreat in the prison) would not be as thorough after two days of entrances and exits. I got through the guard station with shaky knees. Then I had to get the gift into her possession.

JULIA TAUGHT ME THAT "WHAT IS REALLY OF IMPORTANCE AND VALUE IN LIFE IS WHAT YOU HAVE WHEN YOU ARE STANDING NAKED IN A BARREN ROOM."

I would not ordinarily break the rules. Perhaps I was remembering the day I had flown from Texas to Massachusetts to see Julia, and the guards, who knew me, would not let me in because they "couldn't find the paperwork" authorizing my well-planned visit. I had traveled two thousand miles, and I never got inside. Or perhaps it was my small defiance of the horrifying injustices in the system. I don't know. I only know that I had always followed the rules, and then I decided to break them.

The retreat was ending, and guards were positioned around the room, watching. I walked past Julia and whispered to her that at some point before I left I would shake her hand and pass something off to her in that motion. She nodded ever so slightly. I felt as criminal as if I were passing drugs or a colt revolver. What I actually held in the palm of my hand was a small ceramic ornament in the shape of the state of Texas, where I was living at the time. It was a piece of me.

Before I left the room that day, I reached for Julia's hand as planned. We smiled and said good-bye, smoothly transferring the gift from my hand to hers. I watched her slip her hand into her pocket and walk slowly away. She waited until she had returned to her cell to look. She told me afterward that the object itself was irrelevant. It was the risk, and the secret that two hearts shared.

IN THE END, MY SHOWING UP AS OFTEN AS I COULD PROBABLY MATTERED MORE THAN ANY WORDS.

After many denials of parole, Julia eventually moved into a group transitional home. From there she wrote, *"I am a spirit free… a being who is an extension of earth, sea, and sky. No matter how difficult this present situation is, I will extract the goodness that this system tries to suffocate. The full moon a few nights ago was almost a butterscotch color. My thoughts soared out when I saw it.*

"My body may have to go through these motions, but my mind refuses to follow. My spirit absorbs all the fire."

Goodness and truth were like a whisper within the walls of the prison, sandwiched as they were between the more strident roars of harsh realities. *"The night is as bright as the day"* (Psalm 139:12). The mystery of those words, raised against the power of the keys and locks...the brutality of many guards...seemed so impotent. Yet looks deceive. *Something else is at work in life.*

When I met with the women, sometimes there were long periods of silence. They watched me, their eyes scanning my face for signs of pity or judgment. In the end, my showing up as often as I could probably mattered more than any words.

They confessed to me, asked questions I couldn't answer, told stories that may or may not have been exaggerated. And I wondered at the simple fact that our paths had crossed at all. I sat with them in silent communion, knowing I would never be present in such a way with some of my dearest friends. How could that be so? But when a prisoner walked in to see me, I never knew whether I would see her a next time. As far as I knew, we had sixty minutes. And the minutes became our host, the locked door our wine.

77

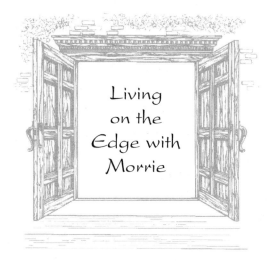

Living
on the
Edge with
Morrie

Opening the door to my office, I poked my head slowly around the corner to see if the man who had asked to meet with me was waiting. I had no formal waiting room, just a cane chair set up in the drab, narrow hallway with a few magazines tossed on the floor beside it. I doubted that anyone ever really flipped through a magazine in that hallway. The lighting was too dim. But at least the offering was made.

In contrast, my little office had two large windows and wonderful light. Its cheerfulness and brightness were always a surprise after the hallway. A love seat with denim and white ticking was set against the right-hand wall. In the middle of the room, facing the love seat, was my own comfortable chair, a large, swiveling circle of bamboo that supported two giant, multicolored cushions. Behind my chair, the white drafting table I used for a desk was usually stacked high with client files and insurance forms. Framed prints of both New York City in wintertime and Monet's water lilies added color to the walls. On the wicker, glass-topped table next to my chair was a well-worn appointment book and the ever necessary digital clock, telling me how many minutes remained in a session.

In retrospect, it's amusing that I was so tentative as I peered around the door into the hallway that day. The man waiting for me was definitely there. The moment he heard the door squeak on its hinges he leapt to his feet, brushing past me in a flurry. Not waiting for any invitation or formalities, he marched into the room with the words, "I knew you were a woman, but I didn't think you'd be so young." The clear implication was, *What could* you *possibly know.* Then he majestically sat down in my chair and fixed two bright, blue eyes on my face, his eyebrows arched, a look of *you'll have to prove yourself to me* in his every gesture.

Hindsight is sometimes a glorious thing. At that moment, neither one of us would have guessed that Morrie

Schwartz was soon to become known to millions by his first name alone, and known to them for his courage and love. This was well before his fame. Before a life-changing diagnosis. Before the amazing opening that would take place within him. Before the two of us had any idea what lay ahead. Before he gave me permission, should I ever decide to do so, to talk about a particular bond we forged and the boundaries we pushed. It was before everything we were about to experience in the crucible of life and death...forgiveness...and letting go. He was there, meeting me in the midst of my busy day, because a former client of mine had suggested that we meet. I had offered him this hour in between clients, when I had a few minutes free.

On that first day I was only annoyed. He seemed rude and he was sitting in my chair. I had never asked someone entering my office to change seats. But I asked Morrie. Really, I *told* Morrie. I held out my arm, swinging it toward the love seat. He got the idea, giving me my little victory. It mattered little. He had only just begun.

The initial interview, *his* interview of me, was priceless.

Do you have a license to practice psychotherapy?

"Of course, Morrie. I couldn't practice without one."

Hmmm. Do you have a master's degree?

I'm irritated, but try not to show it. "Yes. Of course." Stated firmly.

He was small and wiry, with a slightly disheveled look about him. Seventy-eight years old. A full head of white hair, a colorful cotton shirt...but it was obvious that appearance meant little to him. It was not where he placed value.

He leaned in for the kill.

Do you have a doctorate?

"No, I don't. And it's not required."

Yes, but I do!

I didn't reply. I looked at him. He sat forward on the couch, tossing the decorative pillows aside.

Do you see individuals only, or groups as well?

"I only see individual clients."

Well, I work with groups, and it requires greater skill.

I can't believe he's for real. I don't care if he's the most beloved teacher in Boston. I'm not interested. But he's not done.

Are you published?

He's a sociologist, so I know very well what he means. Am I published in scholarly journals, am I bright? Competitive? Knowledgeable? The truth is, I have just published my third book. So I say that. I say that I am the author of three works of nonfiction. Ah. Another notch in his belt.

He glows.

I have authored and coauthored three times as many texts!

For fifty minutes he holds forth. At the end we have learned every way in which he is superior. I'm barely interjecting comments anymore; I'm merely listening to Morrie's monologue. Then with ten minutes left, he asks his next question abruptly.

So, doctor, what do you think?

The words fly from my lips, unedited. I deliver them in an even tone, but I nevertheless deliver them. "I think, sir, that you are possibly the most arrogant individual I have ever met." Morrie startles, abruptly pulling back his head in a manner I would come to know very well, a look and gesture expressing both surprise and the fact that rapid thinking is going on. Then he slaps his hand on his knee and says, *I didn't think you'd have the guts to say it. You may have promise!* He is filled with mirth, absolutely delighted with himself. He laughs out loud and presses on. *And what do you think is wrong with me?*

My response is again immediate, bypassing the mind. The words spill out. "I think you need to open your heart."

I don't say it with an attitude. I say it simply and plainly. But to my great surprise, he bursts into tears. In a second, the space between us has shifted dramatically. He is no longer following a carefully crafted script intended to subordinate me. He has moved without warning to something at his core. I draw a deep breath and sit still, letting the moment sink in. I ask myself: What vein has been struck and where will we go from here? Little do I guess that in the months ahead I will ask myself this question over and over again, with increasing consequence.

─────────── ⟲ ───────────

THE WORDS FLY FROM MY LIPS, UNEDITED. I DELIVER
THEM IN AN EVEN TONE, BUT I NEVERTHELESS
DELIVER THEM. "I THINK, SIR, THAT YOU ARE
POSSIBLY THE MOST ARROGANT INDIVIDUAL I HAVE
EVER MET."

─────────── ⟲ ───────────

In the following year and a half, Morrie's life story will become well known when he grants three interviews to ABC's late night feature, *Nightline,* with host Ted Koppel. *(Nightline* finds Morrie when an Associated Press news article reports on the local talks he is giving about death and dying.) Mitch Albom, a former student of Morrie's now living in the Midwest will see one of the *Nightline* broadcasts. After seeing his old teacher on his television screen, Mitch will impulsively fly to Boston to connect with his beloved mentor one last time.

And that first visit will grow into Mitch's deeply moving book, *Tuesdays with Morrie,* which will not only chronicle their deepening relationship, but will also include the wisdom Morrie longed to impart as he courageously faced death.

Through Mitch's story and Morrie's own words, millions will learn later what I am now hearing for the first time: Morrie's mother died when he was a young boy, and the impact of that deep wound has been far-reaching. Morrie has also been having neurological tests, medical workups. Something is "off" physically, but no test has yet pronounced the source of his vague symptoms. He has moments of feeling slightly off balance. He has fallen. Felt agitated. Fatigued.

I ONLY OFFER THE SENTIMENT THAT SOMETIMES WHEN CLIMBING A STEEP MOUNTAIN, IT'S GOOD NOT TO WALK ALONE.

I offer to help Morrie with grief work, if he'd like to try. He's still not sure of me. *Why do I need you to do that? I'm sure I can figure it out alone.* I shrug. It is, of course, up to him. I only offer the sentiment that sometimes when climbing a steep mountain, it's good not to walk alone. He's visibly skeptical.

A month or two pass, and we're still deciding whether or not he trusts me and whether he even wants to do grief work at all. He hadn't agreed to meet me in the first place for that reason. He came because of a growing anxiety about his mysterious physical symptoms, and because his former student, and my former client, encouraged him to do so. She thought we'd enjoy one another.

Then a phone call changed everything. The awaited test results are back, and it's the worst possible news. Morrie's diagnosis is ALS, a debilitating illness of the neurological system. There is no known cure. Most ALS patients live only a year and a half to two years following diagnosis.

Things change rapidly. My office is on the second floor of a building that has no elevator, and it's becoming difficult for Morrie to manage the flight of stairs. How will I see you? he wants to know. Would you come to my home? I can think of no other solution. I agree, hoping his home is within walking distance of my office, since my daughter and I are sharing a car. I am relieved when I learn that he lives only a mile away. It's doable. I will be his therapist, if this is what he wants.

My first visit to Morrie's home, and I'm standing at the door, waiting for him to let me in. He already moves quite slowly in contrast to the day we met. The homes in his neighborhood are nicely cared for, but simple. Newton, Massachusetts, the garden city, boasts many large, stone and brick homes with extensive landscaping—crushed stone walkways with flowering trees and well-trimmed bushes. Outdoor sculptures. Monuments. But Morrie's street and his own yard are comparatively modest. The lawns and trees are well cared for, but not lavish.

Morrie lets me in and directs me through the living room to his library, where we sit enclosed on every side by books. His passion for scholarship is evident in this room. Books fill all the spaces, floor to ceiling, and papers and more books are stacked all over his desk. The crustiness and challenge of our first encounters is gone. Morrie is only welcoming and appreciative today, seemingly delighted that I'm here and grateful that I was willing to leave my office and come to him.

I take a little while to look around. There is a large, oversized window opposite the reclining chair where Morrie is seated, with another set of windows behind him, so the room is bright. Through the windows, tall New England hardwoods offer an effortless elegance, their leaves a brilliant canopy.

I choose the chair from Morrie's desk and wheel it alongside his recliner. He has something on his mind and is eager to begin. He is about to push the envelope, and he has obviously thought hard about what he will say to me, how he will present his case.

―――――― ⟡ ――――――

THE CRUSTINESS AND CHALLENGE OF OUR FIRST ENCOUNTERS IS GONE. MORRIE IS ONLY WELCOMING AND APPRECIATIVE TODAY, SEEMINGLY DELIGHTED THAT I'M HERE AND GRATEFUL THAT I WAS WILLING TO LEAVE MY OFFICE AND COME TO HIM.

―――――― ⟡ ――――――

First he covers the most immediate challenge, his diagnosis. It is still too large to take in fully; it will require months of breaking it up into pieces small enough to digest. At the moment it's still too arresting. How does a person experience such great and simultaneous changes in both their inner and outer landscapes and yet maintain equilibrium? You have to move slowly. But one primary awareness is unavoidable: *Life is not forever.* More painfully, *this life, my life, is not forever. Everything is temporary. I can no longer delude myself that I have tomorrow and tomorrow and tomorrow. I no longer have the luxury of a future. I have the new reality of this moment.*

Morrie is sobered. There are no more rhetorical questions. There is facing death and all the questions it has raised about life: griefs never mourned, words spoken too infrequently or not at all, feelings withheld, experiences not yet tasted. He is very clear. This is work he wants to do, this inventory of his life. He's more than willing. But there is more. He looks straight into my eyes. "I realize that it will be important to have a therapist help me with all the challenges ahead. Come once a week and do that with me. But I'm also dying."

I know he is leading up to something, but I can't guess what. Morrie's compact frame leans forward with his words, as if to punctuate their intensity. "I need you to come back a second day each week, not as a therapist, but as a human being. On that day, I need you to respond fully to my questions. I need you to walk through this with me with no therapeutic distance. I need all of you to be here. And I need you to say yes to this request."

In time, Morrie would prove to be skilled at turning my insides upside down. If only I'd known, this was merely the first of many ways in which he would press hard against the rules, the boundaries. The boundaries governing therapeutic relationships are clear, well defined, and very important to me. I didn't make exceptions. It wasn't even a debate. "I can't do that, Morrie," I began.

He was ready. "I'm dying," he retorted. "Dying. There isn't time to protect some rule that's crucial in *different* circumstances. We are facing *these* circumstances. And I'm asking you to think larger, to hear one human being's request to another. I'm asking you not to turn away."

IN TIME, MORRIE WOULD PROVE TO BE SKILLED AT TURNING MY INSIDES UPSIDE DOWN.

I left without giving him an answer, but my wrestling with his request had already begun. *When is the circumstance greater than the rule? When does law concede to Spirit?* I felt angry with him for raising the issue at all. I told him I needed some time to think. He pressed. "Come back a second day *this* week, and tell me." He was incorrigible. He also had no idea that since I usually did not have a car, coming even once a week was a sacrifice. It meant a three-hour block of time from my day to walk to his home, see him, and walk back, thus reducing the hours when I could see other clients and earn my living. Now he was asking for a second day. We said good-bye, with me promising to consider what he'd asked. Frankly, I wanted the whole dilemma to disappear. But as I began walking back to my office, I heard myself repeating the sentiment, *I want all of this to go away.* In that moment I realized that Morrie had to be feeling exactly the same way. But he didn't have the luxury of a choice, like I did.

My thoughts during the next days were troubled. I was busy with work, but Morrie's request intruded whenever work didn't keep me fully occupied. The answer was no. That was clear. No exceptions. I didn't need to get in over my head. I didn't want to. I wanted to have the clarity I was enjoying before a seventy-eight-year-old man started pushing me to think of life in a much larger way.

❧

I promised to call Morrie by Thursday to tell him whether or not I would show up on Friday as a human being. Wednesday night was long. I knew what the answer had to be, but I couldn't find peace in refusing him. Why? What flashed before me was the face of a young boy whom I had counseled while I was still in graduate school. Scott was eleven years old, winsome, defiant, and also particularly skilled at pushing up against me. His parents brought him to the university counseling program because he was experiencing angry outbursts at home, in the classroom, and on the playground. His excellent grades were falling, and no one had been able to figure out what was wrong.

When he and I were first introduced I smiled. He looked like a Norman Rockwell creation. Freckles, long reddish blond bangs that swept his eyes, he was an all-American boy. But *he* wasn't smiling because he didn't want to be counseled by me or anybody. His first sentence to me, spoken with a clenched jaw, was predictive: "I don't want to be here, and I'm never talking to you." So there.

It was a rocky experience for a fledgling therapist. For weeks I sat in a small green room with an uncommunicative client while my advisor and peers watched my misery through a one-way mirror. Hard enough to fail at all, but worse to fail so publicly. Eventually my advisor used my agony as an opportunity to talk about clients who were unwilling to change. His words were direct: No one can be helped who isn't ready or at least willing. In truth, Scott's *parents* were the ones who were willing, and they had brought him to work with me with a hopeful eye toward his healing and changed behavior. But Scott himself was not interested at all. My advisor's recommendation was that the therapy be terminated. I'd wished for an end to my miserable struggle, and here it was. These were the words that would set me free.

But when the words were actually spoken I was face to face, not only with my release, but with something else I hadn't realized: I cared deeply about this boy. Yes, I would certainly do poorly in my practicum because of him, but that was a grade. What would *he* be carrying on into his life? That mattered to me. Apparently, given the level of my upset, it mattered a lot.

The try exceeded the rules and became a profound experience of the power of love to invade the human heart.

I was on my advisor's doorstep three days later, early on a Monday morning.

All my feelings poured out in one stream. *Listen, there may be another way. He hates that room. It's not a room for little boys. Please give me a chance to take him away from the room and be with him in another way.*

My advisor was thoughtful and asked what I had in mind. *Walking with him, that's all. When he comes for his therapy, I'll take him for a walk. We'll kick leaves and visit the animals in the agricultural barn at the edge of campus. We'll climb hills. I'll go with him where a boy needs to go.*

And to the credit of an adventuresome mentor, he said all right and agreed to let me give it a try. That try became so much more than techniques of therapy and text-bound lessons about human behavior and theories of personality. The try exceeded the rules and became a profound experience of the power of love to invade the human heart.

Scott and I began to walk together, and we kept walking through three seasons. We always went outside, even in the cold and rain. For the first few weeks there were few, if any, words between us. We merely walked together side by side. When we finally began to speak, it was about trees and rocks and snakes and birds. Boy talk. We ran. We pushed and shoved. We laughed. In the springtime, his mom drove us to the ocean for one of our walks, and that day we collected shells. Earlier, while still meeting inside, we'd made strings of the love beads that symbolized the new consciousness of love sweeping across the country. Now as we walked, we talked about that love...about relationships and about how people affect one another.

I was continually responsible to my advisor and my peers to describe the progress of this unusual relationship, but I never knew what to say. It fell within no category of therapy that I was studying, but clearly it was working. Scott's parents eventually called my advisor to say that he was doing better in school, and his anger was slowly dissolving; he no longer disrupted the classroom, and he was once again full of life. I could not fathom *why* these good changes had come about, but I was grateful. When we finally terminated, the good-bye was emotional for both of us. We had truly encountered one another, he and I. It had not been superficial. We'd let it become real.

❧❧❧

Following my graduate school years, I began working as a counselor at a small community college. While there, I met and married one of the English professors, Roy D'Arcy, and together we imagined our future. I became pregnant almost immediately, and the birth of our daughter, Sarah, assured us that our dreams were coming true. We had no money, an old house that needed lots of work, and a surplus of love. I don't remember anxiety or cross words or even tension. It was easy. We were sailing without trying.

Eighteen months after Sarah's birth I was pregnant again. Thrilled with the news that we were expecting another child, we took a fateful three-hour trip by car from Connecticut to Massachusetts to share the joy with my parents. On the return trip, twenty miles from home, a drunk driver rearranged my future.

Eleven days later I sat before an open grave while Sarah and Roy were lowered into the earth. Then I went back to my parents' home, three months pregnant and shattered in heart and spirit, to see if I could find my way.

Initially there were many visitors, but I was too enveloped by pain to make much effort. Most of the words meant to encourage or support me only made me feel worse. My life fluctuated between anger and heartache. The anger, of course, was only a thin veneer. At best it offered small moments of respite from the wrenching pain. Everything inside of me hurt. Still, it was preferable to experience anger than to swim continuously in the grief.

ON THE RETURN TRIP, TWENTY MILES FROM HOME,
A DRUNK DRIVER REARRANGED MY FUTURE.

One particular Sunday afternoon when I was still recovering at my parents' home, my mother came to my room and told me I had visitors. I greeted that news with a harsh remark, the full force of growing despair expressing itself. My mother rightly left me to my own hardness, telling me to greet my guests or not. She slammed the door behind her.

The slamming of the door got my attention, and I briefly saw myself and the misery I was inflicting all around me. I hated who I was becoming. Chastened, I pulled on a clean shirt and walked into the living room, hoping to listen to the voices in the kitchen until I figured out who was there. To my surprise, there was a man standing alone in my parents' living room, looking out the window toward the bay. He turned when I entered the room, and I stared in disbelief. Neither the intervening years nor his maturation could prevent me from recognizing that face. Same freckles. Same reddish blond bangs, now swept to the side and slightly gelled. Now, clean shaven. But I knew him. I knew him well. Scott.

As I was trying to believe what I was seeing and make sense of Scott's presence, he was already across the room, his full-grown hands extended to mine. "Yesterday I heard about your accident," he explained. "I was at the university and ran into your old advisor. He told me." No response found its way past my level of shock. I couldn't answer him, couldn't form any words. *Oh, my God.* That single thought filled me and kept repeating itself. Here I was, angry, unreachable. And perhaps the one person against whom my heart had no defense had just walked through the door.

He quietly reached out and took my hands in his. "My parents are in the kitchen," he explained. "I begged them to drive down here with me, to help me find you." I watched him, but I still couldn't speak. He went on, "Paula, at the hardest time of my life, you were there for me." His voice dropped to a whisper. "So I wanted to be here for you." He had come to pass back the love.

Scott guided me to the couch where we sat in silence as he continued to hold my hands. His arrival, his walking across that room to hold my broken heart . . . who could measure the meaning of such a gift or the extent of healing it carried? The sheer directness of the love.

And now I realized that Morrie's request was for a similar love. Morrie was saying, please, exceed the boundaries . . . make an exception to the rules. I felt like a lawyer who'd been searching for the compelling legal precedent. Now I'd found it. Step over the threshold, Morrie was saying. Suddenly it was so simple and so clear: I had *walked* with Scott. We walked together. That's what our experience had been. Now Morrie was asking me to walk with *him,* as well, but to walk with him toward death. He was asking me to put aside the rules of convention and play by the inner rules of love.

I called on Thursday morning to say I would be there on Friday, not as a therapist, but as a human being. The phone call took two minutes. What would follow might not be as simple, but there was no longer any question that I would go.

❦

When I arrived on Friday afternoon, Morrie deliberately led me to a small den tucked behind the living area. He was wise. If we were changing the game plan, we should also change the room. Other than Morrie's study, each of the rooms in his home was open and uncluttered, making the few pieces of art and the scattered paintings very distinct. I settled into a small chair opposite Morrie and waited. I didn't need to worry about how this would go. Morrie was in charge.

First question: "Were you raised as a Christian?" I was taken aback, but I probably shouldn't have been. It was a continuation of his initial interview a few weeks ago. But this time the subject matter was my life, not my career.

"Yes," I said carefully, "I was raised in that tradition."

"I was afraid of that," he shot back. "So here are the ground rules: never, ever speak of it. I don't want to hear about Jesus. There was too much anti-Semitism in my upbringing in New York. Understand? The scars are still painful."

I understood. I wasn't intending to initiate conversations anyway. I was only intending to respond, and I said that.

Morrie rushed on. "I'd like to read your *three* books." The inflection made me laugh because the effect was clear: your *three little books, in contrast to my ten or twelve.* That was fine, I'd be glad to bring the books to him, but I questioned out loud whether or not the books might lead to areas he'd just announced he didn't want to hear about. He was unperturbed. "Any book can be closed," he retorted.

He asked some questions about my family of origin, my place in the birth order, and my relationship with my dad, since he, a father, was now thinking about his own relationships with his sons. I kept wondering whether I was passing muster. But I answered everything honestly and fully, even though our format still felt awkward. On Tuesday I had agreed to be his therapist; three days later we were two souls discussing the experience of life. Yet Morrie bridged it gracefully because he wasn't concerned about whether or not I was comfortable. In his eyes, I'd come through the barrier when I agreed to be there for him. He was only intent on the journey ahead.

After that meeting I dropped off my three small books, which he received with a smile.

The books were sitting on the table in front of him when I arrived the following Friday. I saw his first tenderness that day. Holding the copy of *Song for Sarah* in his hands (*Song for Sarah* is the story of the deaths of my husband and first daughter, Sarah), he said, "So this is why you are a good guide through grief." There were tears in his eyes. "I'm sorry," he said. "It must have been hard. You loved her." He looked at me. "You said goodbye after she'd already gone. I have to say good-bye knowing that I'm going."

I was painfully aware of that. And to me it seemed immeasurably more difficult to face saying good-bye in that way. Even though I'd spoken of my loss on stages and in seminars all over the world, sitting with someone face to face who was learning about my history for the first time had a very different character.

Morrie's simple *I'm sorry* touched me, and that day set a tone for the many Fridays to come. Now it was clear. We were going to go all the way into both our lives. No holding back. No niceties. As he kept reminding me, he was dying; there wasn't time to waste.

The playing field was treacherous, yet it also offered the great gift of knowing that our moments were numbered. That's always true, of course. But since the mind refuses to know it, we seldom live from that power.

---⟋◉⟍---

EVEN THOUGH I'D SPOKEN OF MY LOSS ON STAGES AND IN SEMINARS ALL OVER THE WORLD, SITTING WITH SOMEONE FACE TO FACE WHO WAS LEARNING ABOUT MY HISTORY FOR THE FIRST TIME HAD A VERY DIFFERENT CHARACTER.

---⟋◉⟍---

Over a period of time these Friday conversations became a fabric in both our lives. Morrie was fascinated by my weekend travels to lead retreats. Who was there? Why were such deep connections made during those hours? He had me talk about everyone I had met, and he drank in the stories. He ventured, "I wish you had the same look in your eye when you spoke about me. What connects you so quickly to total strangers?"

I laughed. "That about which I am forbidden to speak!"

"I see," he said, but without the familiar frost to his words.

⟋◉⟍

After I had been in Alabama one particular weekend, Morrie said that I was unusually full of life...that my eyes had a different brightness. He demanded the story from the weekend, but I hesitated, finally confessing that telling the story would move closer to an area that felt uncertain to me. I didn't want to offend him or disregard his wishes. I didn't know how he regarded what I considered to be the appearance of Spirit in our ordinary affairs. Maybe he thought it was pure nonsense. He waved off my sentences with the back of his hand, impatient with me. "Tell the story!" he insisted.

AS HE KEPT REMINDING ME, HE WAS DYING; THERE WASN'T TIME TO WASTE.

My friend Marcia organized the retreat. She is an amazing woman, I told Morrie, with a strong, deep heart and faith. Things that tip the scale toward the miraculous will frequently happen when I'm with Marcia. On Saturday afternoon I'd finished speaking and was standing just inside a church pew, autographing copies of my books. As I reached out for the next book being held out to me, I saw a hand extended through the crowd of people pressing toward me. In that hand was a small object that someone obviously wanted me to take. I couldn't see the person, only the hand. I took the offered gift and dropped it into my purse, quickly forgetting that I'd done so. I continued to greet people and sign books until I went on to a special dinner. By the time I reached my hotel the hour was late. I was tired, but I still spent some time preparing the talks I would give during two identical church services the next morning.

The next day I ordered my breakfast from room service and ate yogurt and fruit while going over my notes. I absentmindedly sipped tea. It felt as if I should add something else to my remarks...but what? Only then did I remember that I had dropped something into my purse the day before, and I opened my pocketbook to find it. Stuck to the side pocket was a small square of cardboard. I pulled it out and examined it. Pinned on the cardboard were two tiny bronze baby shoes. Underneath the shoes was a scripture reference, Acts 1:8. I had no idea what that verse was, so I found the hotel Bible and looked it up:

> But when the Holy Spirit comes upon you, you will be given power, and you will be my witnesses in Jerusalem and all Judaea and Samaria and as far as the end of the earth.

I studied the words, then the shoes. And in the next moment, quite unexpectedly, I saw the face of a particular man who'd been in attendance at the retreat all weekend. I was certain, without knowing why, that it was important to give one of the shoes I was holding to him.

I tried to dismiss the thought because it was so silly. The person I was picturing was a large man; what would he do with a tiny shoe? And how would he regard me if I offered it to him? — not to mention how ridiculous it would all seem. I returned to my preparation, but the shoes kept intruding. They seemed to have a life and a will of their own. Apparently nothing else was going to be done until I dealt with them. So I finally resolved to give the shoe to the man if indeed I saw him again that morning.

I arrived just in time for the first service, and I was relieved that the man and his wife were not in attendance. Following the service I counseled with a couple trying to decide whether or not to be married. When I rushed back into the sanctuary it was just before the second, and final, service was ready to begin. I sat down in one of the front pews, but even with my eyes closed it was difficult to screen out the growing activity in the church, especially with latecomers moving in on either side of me. I felt frustrated by the lack of solitude, but it wasn't for any holy reason. My eyes were shut because I was already anticipating my flight back home, trying to figure out how I would ever find the extra twenty-five hundred dollars I badly needed to make a house repair. It was that mundane.

When the organ prelude signaled the start of worship, I opened my eyes and glanced to my right. There sat the very person to whom I had resolved I would give the baby shoe "if I saw him." My stomach knotted. I was really going to be forced to do this. What amazing coincidence, him sitting beside me. But before I could speak, he nodded to his wife, who had moved to the other side of me, and he handed me a small white envelope. I didn't want to lose courage, so I thanked him and said that I had something for him as well. "Open this first," he encouraged. I ripped open the envelope and found a note thanking me for the weekend retreat. It was signed John and Judy Bentley. There was also a folded piece of paper. I pushed back the fold and looked at a check for twenty-five hundred dollars.

I looked first to him, then to his wife, Judy. He spoke first. He said that as he and Judy had prayed that morning, he'd felt led to write me a check. He had no idea whether I was rich or poor, whether I needed the funds or was abundantly wealthy. It didn't matter. His prayer led him to write the check. The first amount he'd written down was two thousand dollars, but something from within corrected him and he changed the amount so it would be twenty-five hundred dollars. That's all he knew. "And you had something for me?" he went on.

But the service was now mercifully beginning. I could hardly give him a miniature baby shoe pinned to a square of cardboard in exchange for that check. The freedom of his gift stunned me. For the next hour it was hard to concentrate, and I was grateful that I'd already given my talk once that morning. As soon as the service ended, I was swept up in greeting people and saying good-bye. Within two hours I'd be flying home. Frankly, I was grateful for the commotion because it allowed me to avoid John and Judy Bentley. Their gift was so great. How would I ever thank them adequately? What could I say?

Marcia and her husband, Audie, had planned to take me to lunch before driving me to the airport. Marcia was keeping track of time, and when she said that we needed to leave, I began gathering my belongings. That's when I heard her ask John and Judy Bentley to join us.

As soon as we'd all been seated in the restaurant, John turned to me. He remembered what I'd hoped he'd forgotten. "Didn't you have something for me?" he asked. There really wasn't much choice. I pulled the baby shoe out of my pocketbook and handed it to this big, strapping man. I stumbled over my words. I told him the story of receiving the two shoes, one of which I was wearing on my lapel. I told him about my strong sense that the second shoe would be meaningful to him in some way. As an afterthought I drew his attention to the scripture reference printed on the card, Acts 1:8.

John listened with emotion, fingering the card in his hands. Acts1:8, he finally said, was the very verse in Scripture that had turned his life around the year before at a men's retreat. Because of that verse, he was now the kind of man who prayed and listened...and wrote checks when the spirit guided him to do so.

The specific meaning of the shoes was still unclear to us. But the importance of the verse was undeniably powerful, to say nothing of John's gift to me of precisely the amount of money I needed. None of us doubted that in time every aspect of this story would make sense. We parted knowing that our lives were irrevocably linked.

Morrie listened with keen attention and then grew pensive. He asked me how I explained such things. "The Spirit of God," I said. I had no other explanation. What else encompasses such mystery and coincidence? Or beauty? Morrie nodded his head, still deep in thought. When he led me to the door he was still pondering the story.

As the weeks passed Morrie's strength declined. His legs weakened noticeably, and soon he moved from cane to walker to wheelchair. Even his arm muscles showed signs of being compromised. The question was always there: What would the future hold? At this same time my friend Pat was a live-in companion to a woman named Helen, a vibrant and beautiful woman in her fifties who also had been diagnosed with ALS. With Pat's encouragement I flew to Dallas to meet Helen and learn what might be ahead for Morrie.

——————— ❦ ———————

MORRIE LISTENED WITH KEEN ATTENTION AND THEN
GREW PENSIVE. HE ASKED ME HOW I EXPLAINED
SUCH THINGS. "THE SPIRIT OF GOD," I SAID.

——————— ❦ ———————

The progress of ALS is different for each person. Helen, although close to death, was still able to walk with a shaky gait. ALS affected her upper extremities first. (It was the opposite for Morrie.) But in spite of her labored breathing and the attendant difficulty she had with speaking, she lovingly and willingly agreed to meet with me. I found the home where she and Pat were staying, and the three of us went to a nearby park for a picnic. The picnic was liquid only for Helen. She could no longer chew or swallow solid food. She graciously let me feed her, raising a cup of liquid to her lips.

It was sobering for me to witness how ALS progressed, and of course Morrie was anxious to know what I had experienced. He and Helen began to communicate via brief notes, and even though they never met, her death was a blow to him. She knew what I could never know, and her encouragement had been a great boost. She, like Morrie, rose to meet the disease with a stunning spirit. And ironically, in their prime, they had both particularly loved to dance. Above all else, Helen wanted me to be sure to tell Morrie that she'd learned to dance without ever leaving her chair. "Tell him it's possible. Tell him I dance every day." By the end, Morrie had learned that secret himself.

❦

I always arrived on Fridays prepared for any conversation or request. But I was still unprepared the morning Morrie looked up and said, "I want you to pray."

"Out loud?" I asked.

He nodded. I took a deep breath. We were a long way from where we'd begun. He said very little after I prayed, but the intimacy of sharing this experience had affected both of us. Morrie was seldom at a loss for words. His next question was always ready. But not on that day. On that day we looked at the trees outside his window, and we talked about the hibiscus plant near his recliner whose blossom was ready to unfold. The unfolding of those blossoms had become a potent sign of the miracle of life for Morrie. He watched them carefully, once calling me to announce the imminent appearance of a new blossom, and wondering whether I could arrive in time to watch with him.

AS MORRIE'S STRONG DETERMINATION TO DIE WELL BEGAN TO CHANGE HIM, THE CHANGE WAS INCREASINGLY VISIBLE.

The next Friday Morrie asked whether I would be willing to join him when his Buddhist meditation teacher came to visit. A Jew by birth, Morrie had maintained a Buddhist practice for years. It shocked him that I immediately said yes. He told me later that he was certain I would decline the invitation.

But the afternoon when his teacher and I were scheduled to meet with Morrie, he was having a choking spell. As time went on, these became more and more common. When it was critical, as it was that day, one of his therapists would arrive to pound on his back until the accumulated mucous had been broken up. Morrie's own chest muscles were too weak for him to do that for himself any longer. While he was being helped, his teacher and I sat in the living room and talked. I was immediately drawn to her, and by the time Morrie was ready to see us, she and I had already established a wonderful rapport, and our two hours with Morrie were delightful. He confessed afterwards that he had fully expected us to have a heated conversation. (Knowing Morrie, he had hoped so.) But there was no divide and no conflict. We all settled on love. Morrie said later that it was amazing to experience a common spring much deeper than the boundaries of our different traditions.

❦

As Morrie's strong determination to die well began to change him, the change was increasingly visible. He grew more and more convinced of the importance of each day, and he began asking me questions about my strained relationship with my father. I didn't always want to speak about it, but Morrie had a way of pressing. His own relationship with his sons was so important to him . . . maybe he felt a mission to push until I too experienced that kind of closeness with my father. At any rate, because of our conversations and his repeated inquiries about whether or not I'd taken any steps forward, I began to visit my father on a regular basis.

Forgiveness and healing became a constant conversation between Morrie and me. In addition to asking me about developments in my relationship with my father, Morrie repeatedly wanted me to retell a story I'd told him about the day I met the drunk driver responsible for the deaths of my family. It had been a defining moment for me, even though I didn't meet him until seven years after the accident. At that time, the driver was subpoenaed as a witness in a civil trial concerning existing highway conditions at the time of the accident. I had never seen or met him before, in any of those intervening years. This was our first meeting. But seven years worth of effort to forgive, to even become *willing* to forgive, culminated in a powerful encounter between us that day. The experience was a forceful lesson. It taught me that the power of forgiveness is not only freeing, but it is one of the highest expressions of love.

So Morrie and I talked at length about forgiveness, especially in regards to my healing the wounds in my relationship with my father. And then the unthinkable happened. Morrie took some detail that he'd gleaned from one of our conversations (I'd answered a particular question of his with a great deal of openness and vulnerability), and he used this knowledge to make a smart remark. I was certain that he'd intended it to be funny. But it hurt deeply.

As soon as his words were spoken, I doubled up inside. I continued with our hour together and left without saying a word, but as I walked back to my office, the force of Morrie's comment found its mark. *I'm not sitting in that room an extra day every week so you can use what I tell you against me,* I thought. I was sufficiently hurt to seriously considered ending the Friday visits. But my friend Eddie, a consistent prayer partner, encouraged me to go back one more time. He also promised to pray during that hour. I'll always be grateful that I sought and heeded his wise counsel.

FORGIVENESS AND HEALING BECAME A CONSTANT CONVERSATION BETWEEN MORRIE AND ME.

My next meeting with Morrie was on our therapy day, but when he met me at the door his face was stricken and he held out his hand and said, "Don't speak. Please, don't say a word." Then he wheeled his chair into our Friday room, and I followed. Once we were inside he wept as hard as I'd ever seen him weep. When he gained some control he could only choke out the words, "I know what I did." I'm aware that printing these words, now, on a piece of paper can't begin to convey their force that day. He said the same words over and over, "I know what I did."

Apparently when I'd left his home on that previous Friday, Morrie immediately knew he had crossed a line...he realized it. But it wasn't a mere insight. He described it as moving through a doorway and over a threshold, suddenly aware of the full impact of every word he'd ever spoken. *We wound one another,* he kept saying. *We could love, and we choose not to.* His sight became so clear, and the consequence of his action so forceful, that it was almost more than he could bear.

For me, it was perhaps the deepest confession and admission of transgression I had ever witnessed.

He begged my forgiveness and asked for another chance. I agreed. But separate from my own personal involvement, the experience of Morrie's intense awareness had great power. I could only relate what I was feeling to something described in the final chapter of C. S. Lewis's *The Great Divorce.* In the story, a group of occupants from hell take a one-day bus excursion to heaven. Once there, they observe a chessboard set on a silver table. The reader is told that the silver table represents Time. The chess-like figures moving to and fro on the board represent human beings, busy with the affairs of their lives. But standing behind the table, watching, are figures that Lewis describes as "a great Presence." And each Presence is the Soul that the chess-like figure truly is, longing to reach the small figure that is caught up in the game on the board.

That afternoon as I listened to Morrie, it felt as if the great Presence watching *him* had gotten through.

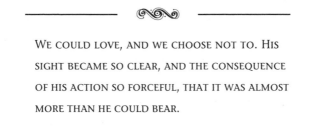

WE COULD LOVE, AND WE CHOOSE NOT TO. HIS SIGHT BECAME SO CLEAR, AND THE CONSEQUENCE OF HIS ACTION SO FORCEFUL, THAT IT WAS ALMOST MORE THAN HE COULD BEAR.

Almost ten years have passed since that morning, and the force of the experience has not diminished. On one level, Morrie's heart had a penetrating awareness of his actions and their consequences. But it was so much more. I watched him be overtaken by a knowledge that permeated his very core, and substantially changed something in his nature. From that moment on, to my eyes, Morrie was different. A commanding compassion had taken over.

A week later, on Friday, master always of surprise, Morrie asked me to tell him anything I understood about the power of Christ. "Not from a book or a Bible," he cautioned. "What do you personally know?" As I talked, Morrie wept. Tears streamed down his cheeks involuntarily, and this response both puzzled and frustrated him. "Why am I crying?" he asked. "I don't even *want* to be moved by what you're saying, and I don't believe it. So why do I cry?"

I didn't know, but I told him what I suspected: that the Spirit hidden deep within us recognizes truths our minds do not consciously know. And in spite of the barriers and limitations *we* impose, in spite of our fears and our refusals, in spite of our determination to limit Spirit to certain names or beliefs ... there is nevertheless a level of awareness within us that exceeds all names and definitions. And this awareness responds from a knowledge the mind does not possess.

We left it at that, and I walked back to my office in a freshly falling snow, thinking that more than anything else, Morrie and I *were* sharing what it means to be a human being, just as he'd requested. We were exploring meaning. We were asking: What does it mean to be alive? Is this human nature our only nature? Is something else trying to emerge? What will we do with the life we were given? How will we live? What limits are we willing to push? How much are we willing to see?

The specter of death was always there. I was able to move in and out of Morrie's home and momentarily forget his diagnosis, but he stayed there. He was living with an unyielding psychic reality: *He was about to die.* In addition, on the mundane level, it was increasingly difficult for him to find a comfortable physical position. I'd assumed that when muscles atrophy and limbs no longer move, there is no pain. But there was considerable discomfort, and the aides would sometimes work for long periods with blocks of cotton or lamb's wool to help Morrie lessen the shooting pains. He always apologized if I had to wait while they positioned him. His consistent awareness of others, even while immersed in such straits himself, was remarkable.

One afternoon that winter I arrived at Morrie's door blanketed with snow. Snow was falling at about an inch per hour, and in the thirty minutes it took me to walk from my office to Morrie's house, I became covered with white. As I hung up my coat and stood shaking out my hat and mittens, Morrie questioned how I could be so wet with snow after just walking from my car to his doorway. That's when he learned that I didn't have a car; my daughter needed the car for afterschool drama rehearsals, and I walked to see him most of the time. The force of that revelation was strong for Morrie. *"You walk here twice a week just because I asked you to? Out of love?"* It hadn't seemed like a big deal to me until I watched Morrie's eyes. Later he would say that knowing that I walked the two miles to his house probably had greater impact for him than any words we ever spoke.

❦

One Friday Morrie asked me to tell him how I'd turned the corner in my own healing. What was the point at which full acceptance of my changed life began? I shrugged and told him that it had been a process, making it extremely difficult to pinpoint a single "aha." Especially now, years later. He looked at me in his direct, inimitable way and said, "I'm dying. Go home and figure it out and return with an answer."

With such a directive from Morrie, I was impressed to go home and figure it out! I reread old journals until I thought I'd found the key he was looking for. Acceptance and healing had begun in earnest for me when I became willing to see beauty in exactly what I'd been given. As soon as I stopped holding on to memories, or even to the way I *wanted* my life to unfold, I began taking in how it *was* unfolding. Morrie listened carefully and then asked, "How do you think this translates to my situation?"

I had anticipated his question, and had an idea. Morrie's memories were not only remembrances of cherished times, but also memories of having a fully functioning physical body. I suggested that we honor together, sense by sense, what it meant to experience life within a human frame. We'd talk about the days when he was fully active. I'd help him remember experiences and events. And then we'd grieve the loss of these abilities and experiences until he felt ready to let the memories go with gratitude and love. It was a process that suited Morrie. He would begin to let go, bit by bit. Since ALS had first affected the mobility in his legs and feet, that's where we began. I prompted him with questions to get us started.

LATER HE WOULD SAY THAT KNOWING THAT I WALKED THE TWO MILES TO HIS HOUSE PROBABLY HAD GREATER IMPACT FOR HIM THAN ANY WORDS WE EVER SPOKE.

What was it like to be a human being and have feet that took you wherever you wanted to go? To dance? To climb mountains? To run? To move from place to place? As Morrie began remembering, tears came easily. He was increasingly aware that being able to walk and move about freely is a great gift. He talked about all the places his feet had taken him, and his memories encompassed both times of pleasure and times of pain. As I listened to him, I looked at my own life. I was borrowing his eyes, which were sharpened by the imminence of death and loss. Morrie told stories and cried and remembered until he was ready to say, "I'm grateful to have known this joy, and I accept the fact that this experience is no longer mine. I let it go with gratitude."

Sense by sense, week after week, Morrie said good-bye to the gift of life. His hands. *Where had they been? What had they held, touched?* Now he was seeing, clearly and powerfully, the potential within each of us to heal or express love through touch. Then he posed a different question. What had his hands *not* touched? That question generated a strong response, similar to the moment when he'd hurt me with a biting remark. This time, a man who could no longer move his hands at will wondered why he'd missed even one opportunity to reach out when he was able to do so.

Because of these absorbing conversations, I walked around freshly aware of how stunning it is to be alive, to be human for a short while...to touch skin, to touch life...to be able to hold one another. Even more striking was my growing realization that the nature of this human experience was up to me. Would I be driven by anger? Stubbornness? Fear? Protection? Love? *Choose the one you want*, as Morrie would say. He was busy choosing the way he wanted to die.

SENSE BY SENSE, WEEK AFTER WEEK, MORRIE SAID GOOD-BYE TO THE GIFT OF LIFE.

He looked down at his own hands, no longer able to do his bidding, and he let go with great thanks.

We shifted to hearing. The song of a bird. The resonance of the human voice. The familiar intonation of someone you love. Music. Morrie played Puccini at full volume, and wept for the beauty of sound and the fleetingness of the experience. He played *Madame Butterfly*, Maria Callas, Vivaldi's *Four Seasons*. And he wept, knowing that the brief lifetime during which we are able to listen to such sweetness is hardly long enough. He listened and remembered until he could say, "I'm grateful to have *ever* heard. The gift was profound. Now I let it go with gratitude."

Vision. The hibiscus plant in Morrie's study. Once he'd ignored it, now it was more than beautiful to him. Nature hadn't held much interest for him when he was walking about, but now that his field of vision was limited to what he could see from his window and what could be brought inside, sight acquired new meaning. He wondered whether he'd see another snowfall. He looked at human faces with renewed focus.

THE NATURE OF THIS HUMAN EXPERIENCE WAS UP TO ME. WOULD I BE DRIVEN BY ANGER? STUBBORNNESS? FEAR? PROTECTION? LOVE? *CHOOSE THE ONE YOU WANT*, AS MORRIE WOULD SAY. HE WAS BUSY CHOOSING THE WAY HE WANTED TO DIE.

By the time we explored the sense of taste, Morrie could no longer swallow easily. He was now drinking only liquids, just as Helen had done when I'd visited her in Texas. But in terms of *our* process, Morrie became very creative. Unable to do his own tasting, he instructed me to go out and find tiramisu and eat it *for* him. We laughed about the number of things a person tastes during a lifetime. For Morrie, there were many tastes that he'd loved. Duck well prepared, potato latke...we laughed until we both cried because they seemed so incongruous when listed together. And then, grateful for the gift, he let it go. We moved to the sense of smell, and Morrie talked about the scent of a pale yellow rose, the fragrance of rhododendrons. And lest it all sound too sublime and soulful, it was all, always, interspersed with Morrie's devilish nature and sharp wit, with his humor and irreverence. In the thick of the most poignant remembrances, I arrived one Friday to be greeted by a string of directives from Morrie. *Please shut the door right now. Move this. Fix that. Sit down.*

I finally had had enough. "Morrie, you're still telling me what to do," I complained.

The right eyebrow arched and the eyes danced. He cocked his head. "And you're still doing it," he declared emphatically. Vintage Morrie.

When the remembrances had all been spoken, we decided to give one another a last gift, something to commemorate this journey. I gave Morrie the small string of love beads I'd made with Scott during the extraordinary year we'd spent walking together. Then I told him about Scott. His eyes misted. The beads had moved from the hands of a young boy to those of an old man. I had my own feelings. I'd been lucky enough to walk with both of them. Morrie's gift to me was from his bookshelf. A worn and treasured copy of Martin Buber's *I and Thou,* a book whose pages encompass the relationship that exists between a human being and the transcendent God.

MORRIE'S GIFT TO ME WAS FROM HIS BOOKSHELF. A WORN AND TREASURED COPY OF MARTIN BUBER'S *I AND THOU,* A BOOK WHOSE PAGES ENCOMPASS THE RELATIONSHIP THAT EXISTS BETWEEN A HUMAN BEING AND THE TRANSCENDENT GOD.

Throughout these months I had been working on the manuscript for my fourth book, which would become *Gift of the Red Bird.* In the book I describe the vision quest I made in the desert in south central Texas. Morrie kept telling me to hurry. He so wanted to read this story, and he was afraid he wouldn't live past the date of publication. Characteristically, he pushed me to bring the manuscript to his house and read it to him ahead of time, just in case. We set aside one particular afternoon, and I did read Morrie the unedited pages.

In the story, a red cardinal guides and befriends me as I confront both myself and my fears in the wilderness. In uncanny and powerful ways, the bird continues to show up throughout my three days and nights and becomes for me an unquestioned sign of God's presence and protection. When I finished reading, Morrie voiced his skepticism. His reaction surprised me since he'd been in tears when I read about the bird's uncanny appearance following a stormy night. Ever the scientist, ever questioning, he finally asked, "Do you truly believe that such things have meaning? That the occurrences are not by total coincidence?"

It was a lovely moment. I turned to the window, and Morrie followed my gaze. Only then did he see what I had been watching for the last ten minutes. A red cardinal was sitting at his windowsill, looking in at us. It had arrived as I read about its appearance in the story. Even Morrie was impressed.

❧

"Don't push the river," says my friend Richard Rohr. Don't get ahead of your soul. The goal isn't to get somewhere. The goal isn't about forcing something to happen. The goal is to be in harmony with the gifts that are already given. The goal is to fall into your life.

I watched Morrie fall into his life. I watched him move from the resolution made by a defiant nine-year-old boy angry at God for taking his mother . . . through the scientist's certainty that "the need to find God is only a desperate attempt to preserve the ego"...to the old man who proclaimed that "nothing really matters but love." Bit by bit Morrie let go of the things that didn't matter and learned that his dignity came from his inner self.

When Ted Koppel interviewed Morrie for a third and final session on *Nightline,* Morrie summed up his philosophy with these words: *Compassion, love, responsibility, and awareness. And we all learn it too late. If we could only see things the way they are, rather than the way we want them to be.* It reminded me of the words of author Stephen Levine, "We bury the very things that might set us free."

The greatest letting go, of course, is the ultimate letting go of life. "How would you approach it?" Morrie wanted to know. I didn't know. "It's not something you can simulate," I told him. "You can't imagine the imminence of death when you're still convinced that you have time." But characteristically, Morrie pressed.

"Well," I ventured, "I think I'd imagine a pair of outstretched arms, into which I'd fall when I was ready."

"You believe a person can determine when they're ready to go?"

"Maybe. Many have done so. If you're no longer holding on, and are willing to let go, what would stop you?"

Morrie was thoughtful. Then alert. "Whose arms would those be?"

It made me laugh. Clearly, he would debate theology to the end. But that was Morrie. It was the uniqueness of his spirit. "Morrie," I said, choosing my words with care, "the name by which your mind knows those arms isn't the point. Your spirit knows. Frankly, I think the name is secondary. It's the falling into them that is so difficult."

"Well," he wanted to know, "if those arms *were* a name I didn't speak, and couldn't recognize, would they still catch me?"

I drew a deep breath and decided to give a simple, one-word answer. "Yes. That's what I believe. Yes."

THE GREATEST LETTING GO, OF COURSE, IS THE ULTIMATE LETTING GO OF LIFE. "HOW WOULD YOU APPROACH IT?" MORRIE WANTED TO KNOW.

Morrie could never leave it there. "Why?"

"Because in the act of falling back, your heart would be fully open and trusting, finally abandoned to Spirit."

In the weeks that followed, Morrie asked me dozens of times to tell him the story of falling back into the outstretched arms. He always closed his eyes when I talked.

"Just picture going to sleep," I would say. "You've let go of everything. There's nothing left to stop you. Let go and you'll be caught."

I visited Morrie for the last time on a Thursday evening in November. His family had called to say that he was weakening. He was in a hospital bed by now, and one eye opened slowly when I came into the room. He smiled weakly as I took his hand. "Tell the story," he mouthed. His words were barely intelligible, but I knew what he was asking because he had asked so often. I told him the story and then sat with him as he slept. When the attendant returned to check on him, I looked back one last time and left. Ultimately that sleep continued, deepening into the coma that carried Morrie away. He died on Saturday morning, serenely and peacefully, just as he had hoped to do.

IN THE WEEKS THAT FOLLOWED, MORRIE ASKED ME DOZENS OF TIMES TO TELL HIM THE STORY OF FALLING BACK INTO THE OUTSTRETCHED ARMS. HE ALWAYS CLOSED HIS EYES WHEN I TALKED.

His funeral was held at Brandeis University, where he'd taught with such enthusiasm and life. Hundreds of young men and women were guided by his knowledge, and they came at the end to pay their respects. I was in Connecticut when Morrie's wife called to tell me he had died, so I had a two-hour car ride in which to sort through my own feelings. Morrie had challenged me. He pushed me to break the rules, and he gave me the opportunity to look through his eyes, *with him,* at his approaching death. My last emotion was gratitude.

⁂

Morrie and I had an important conversation when his life first began to change dramatically, thrusting him into the public eye. He had just taped the first of three interviews with Ted Koppel for *Nightline,* and the response had been overwhelming. Because of *Nightline,* Mitch Albom reappeared in Morrie's life and was beginning to meet with him on Tuesdays to write a book about Morrie's death and dying. As all of this was unfolding, Morrie sat me down. He'd done a lot of thinking, and he wanted me to be honest with him.

Would I be hurt, he wanted to know, if his public interviews and his book with Mitch didn't mention the journey he and I were taking together? Our therapeutic sessions, of course, would never be revealed. That was not at issue. But the Friday journey was separate. In fact he *wanted* me to share that journey, once he died, hoping our experiences might offer solace or perhaps guidance for others. But while his life was still being lived out, it was something he wanted to keep private. His life was already turned inside out...so much of it given away. *"If I give this too,"* he reasoned, *"I'm not sure it will have the same integrity. I need to have something that still belongs only to me. Something I'm living, but not revealing."* I understood, and I agreed. It was similar to writing entries in your diary thinking that one day those thoughts would be published. The honesty of the writing would be immediately compromised.

MORRIE HAD CHALLENGED ME. HE PUSHED ME
TO BREAK THE RULES, AND HE GAVE ME THE
OPPORTUNITY TO LOOK THROUGH HIS EYES, *WITH
HIM*, AT HIS APPROACHING DEATH. MY LAST
EMOTION WAS GRATITUDE.

From time to time over the past decade, and mostly in retreat settings, I have spoken about my "human being" conversations with Morrie. There has always been a strong response.

Morrie was walking a road we will all walk, and the choices he faced are common to everyone. We all decide the extent to which we'll open our hearts. We decide whether or not life is an incomparable gift. We decide how gracefully and fully we'll respond to disappointment and loss, or whether we'll finally yield to the things that cannot be changed. Morrie stood at an inner threshold and decided to cross, reaching for a deeper love. As I finally put this story into words, allowing it to find its way to larger places, I'm aware that I'm doing exactly what I watched Morrie do. I'm letting go, this time for both of us.

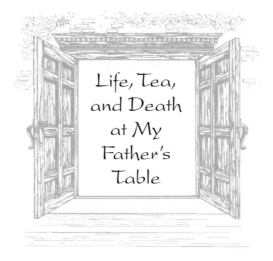

Life, Tea,
and Death
at My
Father's
Table

Because Morrie was urging me to do so, I began visiting my father on a regular basis. His voice was always in my ear. *Resolve things. Get it right now, before it's too late.* One particular evening was especially poignant. My father was having surgery the following day, and I had come to spend the night and drive him to the hospital early the next morning. In the middle of the night I heard him walking around. He couldn't sleep. I crept downstairs and stood in the doorway between the living room and the kitchen. My father was standing next to the kitchen table, the fingers of his right hand spread on the edge of its smooth surface. He didn't hear me, so I stayed in the shadows and watched. He was a short man, bald, with a distinctive hook in his nose, the result of a break that had never been set. His hands were small and thick, but even so, he played piano easily and well, with the lightest touch. When he played he stared into the distance, his eyes dark and unfathomable.

He was deep in thought when I entered the room that night, and I wondered what he was thinking. He walked to the large window at the head of the table and looked out at the moon. I asked myself whether he'd be alive in twenty-four hours to see the moon again. Was he asking the same thing? Then he moved slowly toward the living room, and I stepped back into the shadows. He stopped in front of the large, white recessed bookshelves that filled the right-hand wall and picked up the framed pictures of his children and grandchildren that were displayed there. He held them, one by one.

The moment was sad and discomforting. I was already deep in the throes of life and death with Morrie. Now I was watching my own father face his mortality. But it was easier with Morrie because there was no history. In this house there was not only history, but a difficult one. There were resentments and misunderstandings. For whatever reason, my father had found it very difficult to express approval and love, and our family lived with the tension of the strong emotions that warred inside him. But since we could never name them, or see them, we remained impotent against an invisible world he kept secreted deep within.

And there I was, in the middle of the night, wondering what I had always wondered. What was he feeling? And how could I bridge the distance between us? Was there some way to approach his hidden self? I finally made myself visible and asked him if he'd like to talk or have a cup of tea. He shook his head, no, but neither one of us moved. We were both facing the bookcase, looking in the same direction, standing side by side. I cautiously raised my hand and let it touch his shoulder. He still didn't move, so I began rubbing his back. Little, circular motions. Small patterns that contained a lifetime of longing, traced on his robe. He didn't respond, but he didn't pull away. At least he wasn't alone, and maybe that mattered.

We drove to the hospital early the next morning, and my father was prepped for surgery. When my mother and I rejoined him, he lay shivering on a gurney, waiting to be wheeled into the operating room. His prostate was enlarged, and there were malignant tumors in his bladder. He looked so disempowered in this setting. Was this the tyrant? The man whose moods commanded the household . . . the stern authority who listened to no one?

I stood beside him, my insides churning. I couldn't bear his vulnerability, his nakedness.

I found a nurse and told her that my father was cold. She immediately brought a heated blanket and placed it over his thin hospital gown. I tucked the blanket around his feet and moved back to his side. He smiled his thanks and reached up to squeeze my hand, and there was perhaps more intimacy in that gesture than had ever passed between us. Even when the anesthesiologist appeared to give the shot that would put him out, he didn't let go. Finally his eyes closed, but I didn't step aside until they asked me to leave. I leaned over and whispered *Don't be afraid,* but the drug had already taken effect. As soon as the gurney was out of sight, I raced for the restroom and heaved out my insides. It felt as if I were heaving out all the pain my heart had ever held.

My father survived his surgery, and as he recovered I made an important determination. My focus (my selfish focus) had always centered on my disappointment that our relationship was so limited. That we couldn't speak to one another. That I never knew if he was pleased or displeased. I felt cheated. He was not a demonstrative man. He was not the kind of father I needed. Over the years I gave great power to my complaints, and I allowed my disappointment to justify extended periods when I wouldn't visit or call. I simply stayed away.

Now it occurred to me that my father may not have been an expressive, loving father…but I had not been a particularly loving daughter, either. The pain went both ways. He got cheated too. I remembered visits when I had barely acknowledged him…or when I spoke with animation to my mother, but never looked toward him. Some of Morrie's words pushed at me: *If only we could see people the way they are, and not the way we want them to be.*

My father was a real person, and I had never seen that person. I measured whoever he truly was against the image in my mind. I laid out my conditions. He didn't even need to show up. No wonder he hadn't. I was wed to the father I wanted. And now, at this late date, what if I withdrew those conditions? Was it possible to relate to my father without imposing my own expectations? What if I began visiting him seeking *nothing*… only visiting because that's what I'd chosen to do…because that's the person, the daughter, I wanted to be. I was no longer a child. I needed to grow up and behave like the grown woman I was. I needed to love.

Realistically, I knew that visiting my father more regularly would bring mixed results. Sometimes it might feel good. At other times I assumed it would continue to be difficult. But I now saw that my father's behavior was irrelevant to this venture. His actions had to cease being a condition of *my* loving. My loving had to be in my own hands. It occurred to me with a real start: *Any love dependent on someone else's behavior wasn't love in the first place.* Did I want to *be* loved or did I want to love?

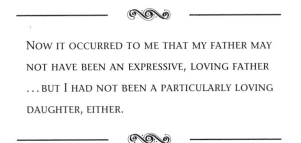

NOW IT OCCURRED TO ME THAT MY FATHER MAY
NOT HAVE BEEN AN EXPRESSIVE, LOVING FATHER
. . . BUT I HAD NOT BEEN A PARTICULARLY LOVING
DAUGHTER, EITHER.

I began using the hour-long drive back to my parents' home to think about love, and to think about the person I wanted to be. One cost of loving without expectation was giving up blame. I was no longer a child dependent on someone else's care. What *had been* was past. Was I really willing to let my first, limited understanding of love be the final say, defining how I would love today? It was a choice. My father's purpose in life was not to match *my* inner image of a father. In fact, his purpose in life was no business of mine at all. I had my own purpose to tackle. I had to let a greater love begin to inform my heart.

After making weekly visits for two months, something shifted. I no longer rated my visits as good or bad.

I stopped feeling happy or sad based on my father's mood. I went to see him because I wanted to. Sometimes he seemed appreciative, and sometimes not. It mattered less and less, until it didn't matter at all.

Having removed my own needs and expectations from the equation, all that remained was the person who was my father, and I began to see that person. I discovered a man for whom life had not been particularly happy and someone limited in making the connections with others that yield fullness and meaning. I saw his frailty, and the fear and insecurity that were his inner demons. And I wished, with all my heart, that his experience of life and work and family could have been so much more. I'd spent over forty years feeling sorry for myself and holding grudges. The truth was that until now, even though we'd lived in the same house, I'd never seen my father at all.

In the final months of my father's life, just before his care demanded a nursing facility, we sat at the kitchen table whenever I came to visit. The kitchen had always been the center of our home. Conversations began and ended around the table. Made from a beautiful golden oak, the table originally had two leaves that were kept in the closet, ready to insert for company. On Sunday afternoons when I was growing up, the extended family would visit. Aunts, uncles, cousins. We gathered around the table with coffee and pastries, soda for the kids. When the children grew restless we'd run off to play, but the adults would sit and talk for long hours. The table was sturdy, with thickly grooved spindle legs that my father set on casters to make it easier to move.

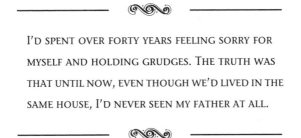

I'D SPENT OVER FORTY YEARS FEELING SORRY FOR MYSELF AND HOLDING GRUDGES. THE TRUTH WAS THAT UNTIL NOW, EVEN THOUGH WE'D LIVED IN THE SAME HOUSE, I'D NEVER SEEN MY FATHER AT ALL.

I vividly remember the day he decided to permanently glue the leaves into place and cover the oak top with Formica, which was the new technology. The act was utilitarian, without question...and over the years the Formica made quick work of spills. But the golden hued oak was art and beauty, and covering it up never settled well in my heart.

At that table we grew as a family, and mealtime was central. During those years whole families still gathered for dinner each evening. There were no conflicting sports schedules or afterschool activities that ran late. Everything ended in time for families to come together.

Even as a cheerleader, I don't remember missing dinner because of an evening game. I don't even remember rushing.

------- ❦ -------

THE KITCHEN HAD ALWAYS BEEN THE CENTER OF OUR HOME. CONVERSATIONS BEGAN AND ENDED AROUND THE TABLE.

------- ❦ -------

But the fact that we weren't rushing didn't mean our life was idyllic. We merely had longer "in house" hours in which to create havoc with one another. Great scenes took place at the table. My usual seat at the far end placed me opposite a large window. I loved sitting there because I could make faces at my reflection in the glass. My antics inevitably caused one of my sisters to laugh so hard she would be sent from the table. That never made sense to me. I was the instigator, and my parents sent *her* away, not me. They never even changed my seat. But why would I point out that error?

At that table my father reviewed our report cards, helped us with math formulas, and delivered many a stern lecture. He was Italian, and even his conversational tone could feel like he was yelling. When he was displeased and being emphatic, the perception was doubly true. I was always scanning his face for signs of approval.

At that table my mother quizzed us on the questions in our Baltimore catechisms. Who made the world? *God made the world.* Why did God make us? *To know, love, and serve him in this world, and be happy with him forever in the next.* My mother wasn't even Catholic; she was Baptist. But she remained faithful to her promise that we'd be raised in the Catholic faith.

We sat at that table with friends, or when our dates were nervously being scrutinized by my father. We sipped tea there, late at night, if our stomachs were upset or we simply couldn't sleep. I sat at that table with Roy D'Arcy when he asked my parents for my hand in marriage. A year later we sat there together, presenting my parents with their first grandchild, Sarah. We bathed Sarah in a large, blue aluminum tub that we set on the table's broad surface.

I returned to that same table three years later, trying to make sense of Roy's and Sarah's deaths. And once my second daughter, Beth, was born (I was pregnant with Beth at the time of the accident), that's where I brought her. She too was bathed in the familiar blue tub. She too felt the familiarity and safety we'd all known in that space.

My father has now died, but my mother still lives in our original family home and the table is there, silent witness, still, to our meals, our conversations, our sadness, and our joy. But it has become a symbol to me of so much more. It represents the very traditions with which I was raised, and it serves as a reminder that in spite of the struggles we experienced in that home, Love was present. In the midst of discord and confusion, Love was at work. Neither our disappointments nor our limited grasp of Love were ever intended to be as far as we would advance. The life lived at that table was meant to be our starting point. But we had to grow beyond it.

LOVE INSISTS THAT EVERYTHING BE SET FREE.

All along the way, ablaze in mystery and paradox, a larger Love waits to set us free. That was the Love that helped me recognize the restricting power of my expectations, and set me in the direction of real change. In a sense it heaved the Formica off my childhood table. The Formica had served a utilitarian purpose for a time. But ultimately, the leaves had to be unglued again, and the golden oak was exposed. Love insists that everything be set free.

One night I dreamed that I walked into my childhood kitchen. My siblings, my mother, my daughter, Beth, were all there. But the table was gone. Vanished. We stood in the space where it had been, and the space had power. In the dream I understood that the former things had been intentionally cleared away. They had to be. All the old ways of perceiving and knowing were going to be replaced. In the great space where the table had once been was room for Spirit to move.

Everything
Lies
before Us

Scott, the young boy with whom I walked when I was a therapist in training, is now middle-aged, with children of his own. I am still stunned by the way we came full circle, encountering one another during two seasons of our lives, both times with such significance. In granting permission for this story to be told, Scott wrote: "All the memories are positive and endearing. Thanks for caring so much and for walking with me."

John Bentley, to whom I gave the baby shoe pin, has remained in my life. John and his wife, Judy, eventually met my daughter, Beth, and Beth immediately loved them as I do. Our mutual friend, Marcia, repeated the story of the shoe and the Scripture verse to friends one day, and a woman who was listening timidly said, "I was the person who gave Paula the shoe." She explained that she often kept small items in her purse to give away, and on that particular day the baby shoes were all she had. Even though she felt strongly encouraged to offer them to me, she struggled against her impulse. It seemed cruel to give two little shoes to a mother who had two daughters, one of whom had died. But she decided to trust what was guiding her and reached her hand through the crowd that day.

Within a year following this experience, I stayed with John and Judy while passing through Alabama. They awakened me in the morning and told me that they intended to pay fully for Beth's college education. Their hearts had been impressed to do so. John said, "You will never see another tuition bill." And I didn't. They were taking seriously the Scripture admonishing believers to take care of the fatherless and the widows. They also explained that they needed to learn to give, not from their surplus, but at a cost.

In time, John sat down and told Beth the story of the baby shoe and gave it to her. So the shoe is now passed on. He assumed a fatherly role that day, and he sent her out to explore the far corners of the world.

Julia, the young woman I met in prison, has now been released. Three days after Thanksgiving, in November 2003, I stood at the Newton Center train station in Massachusetts, waiting for the train from Boston to arrive. The train pulled into the station at precisely 12:30 p.m., and Julia stepped off. A moment we'd imagined and dreamed about for many years was happening. Her sentence had been served. Julia was free.

─────────── ⚬ ───────────

THEY ALSO EXPLAINED THAT THEY NEEDED TO LEARN
TO GIVE, NOT FROM THEIR SURPLUS, BUT AT A COST.

─────────── ⚬ ───────────

It seems natural that we might have shed tears, but in fact, we laughed. We hugged one another and whirled around in a circle and laughed and laughed. No guards. No metal detectors. No restrictions. We found a small Indian restaurant and talked nonstop. We talked about the ceramic piece I had smuggled into the prison retreat years ago. We talked about some of the inmates I'd come to know. We talked about the remarkable fact that she was about to enter the School of Divinity at Boston University. There was not enough time to say all the words and express all the feelings.

After our meeting in Boston, Julia e-mailed to say that she'd spoken with her lawyer and learned that she will be denied a driver's license for the rest of her life. She *could* appeal and insist on a hearing, but the lawyer told her that the fight would be financially prohibitive, and she'd lose in the end anyway. She was philosophical in her e-mail. "They want my license more than I do, so I think they should have it," she wrote. "Solzhenitsyn has a great saying: *You can have power over people as long as you don't take everything away from them. But when you've robbed a man of everything, he's no longer in your power.* Well, I'm saving myself the step of getting robbed—I'm passing go and collecting more freedom. And in a few minutes I'll be on my way to work—*walking* along the river."

I vividly remember the first night I visited Julia's prison. I thought I would be helping others. I told myself that I was bringing something of value to those less fortunate. I was so ill informed. The truth is that I had no idea how much I needed to be there, and how much would be given to me. The experience inside the prison was a mirror in whose glass I saw the reflection of many things.

There have been a number of prisons and shelters since then. Men and women of remarkable honesty have given me a glimpse of their courage. Every story reminds me of how little I know about freedom, and how the greater Love differs from the love we pursue.

Along the way I've learned that we avoid our own healing at great cost. Until the work of forgiveness is begun, until we learn the language of gratitude, until we understand the small nature of much that we call love, until we realize the power of imagination and begin to picture what we want to create, we will repeat the same patterns and miss the portals that might set us free. The old dynamics are too compelling, the familiar ideas and beliefs too ingrained.

Thresholds demand a willingness to walk in new directions. They ask us to "not know" — we who are so in love with knowing. They insist that we be led where we never intended to go. They will not respect the hunger that feeds the ego and keeps us small. They speak of a Love far different from the one we know. They call to us awaken from sleep and see the world for the first time.

Some say there's a kind of detachment to the truest love. That this is its nature. And that when the full power of Love is unleashed, even the stars are affected. I remember a moment when I was leading a Women's Rite of Passage at Ghost Ranch in New Mexico. When we met on the first morning, we discovered a bird trapped in a long plastic sleeve in front of one of the windows.

It was flailing wildly, looking for the way out. It was clear that we would not proceed until the bird was freed. Every woman in the room understood the symbolism. The wings of the bird were our own.

As I work on my final manuscript revisions, WOMEN-SPEAK 2007 is in the final nine months of gestation. Time seems suspended and we move in increasing awareness that the day of the event is no different than this present day. In fact, not being able to experience the latter, we will miss the former. They are identical. The blazing genius of artist Mary Southard has given us a visual picture of our vision: Women of every race in flowing robes, hands outstretched above their heads, while the earth spins overhead. She calls the painting, *Women Singing Earth*.

Will I unsettle my life in order to grow? Do I really want to know where Love can take me? Can I leave home in order to know what is true? Can I let Spirit awaken my sleeping soul?

Acknowledgments

The entire team at Crossroad Publishing has been an integral part of this book. In ways large and small they have each contributed to this manuscript's emergence, and I am immensely grateful for the growing we've done together. My appreciation to Maria Devitt, Jackie Andre, Matthew Laughlin, Christine Phillips, Jim Phillips, and especially John Jones. Although John is not my assigned editor, he is an incredible support, and always right there, at a moment's notice, to talk through ideas, or share his unswerving belief in things. Just to think of him makes me glad. I greatly thank Gwendolin Herder, who is both my publisher and friend. Her openness, honesty, and willingness to listen have helped me turn significant corners as a writer.

I am grateful to my editor Roy M. Carlisle. Roy is a gifted editor who continually opens up new vistas and says to me, "You can do this. Go for it." He has affected how I look at many things, what I think is possible, how I view myself as a writer, and what I am willing to risk. His love of books and his commitment to authors is notable.

Thanks to my mother, who died so suddenly as this book was about to be printed, to my late father, to

Acknowledgments

Scott, to Julia, to Morrie, to John and Judy Bentley, to Marcia Hodges, and to Pat Simmons, for the strong and wonderful stories that changed all our lives. They remind me that *this is it,* that no moment should be wasted, that the short journey we call a lifetime is filled with power.

I thank Robin and Jamshid Galehzan for their companionship ever since I arrived in California. In particular, I thank Robin for listening to the story of this book as it unfolded, adding her keen insights, and patiently and lovingly helping me get my bearings. I thank Jamshid for teaching me about the beauty of the poetry which threads its way through his culture in Iran, and for being an exceptional model of the power of a quiet and loving presence.

Grateful appreciation to Tony and Pam Petrotta, Jack Mingo and Erin Barrett, McNair Wilson, and Daphne Drescher for also opening their arms to a newcomer in their midst. Each of them made me feel immediately welcome in California by filling my life with good food, music, and laughter, as well as runs on the beach and around the lake.

Thanks to Madeline Tyng for once again taking photographs for me, and for the extraordinary way she allows me to share in her own recent loss of her husband, Tom.

Her beauty and strength, even in grief, convince me that we *are* capable of so much more in our relationships.

Special appreciation to my dear friends Kaye Bernard, Denise Casey, Lisa Levy, Tom and Debbie Morrill, Connie Barrios and Stacey Dille for all the things they so willingly do to help me further both my speaking and the ministry of my Foundation.

And deepest thanks, always, to my daughter Beth, who is such a bright light in my world.

About the Author

Paula D'Arcy, a writer, retreat leader, and conference and seminar speaker, travels widely in the United States, Canada, and abroad. She is also president of the Red Bird Foundation, which supports the growth and spiritual development of those in need and furthers a ministry both to those in prison and those living in third world or disadvantaged cultures.

A former psychotherapist who has ministered to those facing issues of grief and loss, Paula worked with the Peale Foundation, founded by Dr. Norman Vincent Peale, from 1980 until his death in 1993. In recent years she has frequently teamed with Fr. Richard Rohr in presenting seminars on the Male/Female Journey. Her individual work includes leading women in Initiation and Rites of Passage.

Paula's ministry grew from personal tragedy. In 1975 she survived a drunk driving accident which took the lives of her husband and twenty-one-month-old daughter. Pregnant at the time, Paula survived the accident to give birth to a second daughter, Beth Starr.

A Word from the Editor

The Crossroad Publishing Company seeks to contribute to the richness of life with fine books as a leader in spiritual, religious, and cultural publishing. We value the people with whom we work, our colleagues and our authors, all of whom we welcome as partners in our common venture.

In the more than twenty-five years that I have been a part of this "common venture," the ground of publishing has shifted dramatically. And in many ways Paula D'Arcy is an exemplar of that shift. Allow me to explain. For many years writers and publishers were confined to the narrow straits of the denomination to which they belonged. So a book by a Methodist or Baptist or Presbyterian or Episcopalian or Roman Catholic clergy or layperson was published by that particular denominational publishing house. And it was read by laity or clergy in that particular denomination. This was generally true for every denomination, Protestant or Catholic, large or small, including the lesser known stepsisters such as evangelicals and pentecostals.

In the sixties and seventies a major shift began. The mainline denominations were losing members; all kinds of other movements were growing *across* denominational lines. Clergy and laity were shifting their allegiance from dying denominations to vital movements.[1] In other words the mode or particular way in which each person worked out their salvation and spirituality became primary. If their spiritual path was dominated by social action or contemplation or biblical study or charismatic experiences or liturgical practices, then those people "felt" closer to others who were so inclined, even if they were in other denominations. Although invisible, these lines of allegiance were not only profound but would change the religious landscape in this country forever. Religious publishing — magazine publishers figured this out before book publishers did—had a harder time following this shift, but it tried.

Enter writers like Paula D'Arcy, who had the ability to cross denominational lines because of their particular emphasis. One of my own mentors, Richard J. Foster, has outlined his paradigm for these emphases in spiritual life as follows: the contemplative tradition, the holiness tradition, the charismatic tradition, the social justice tradition, the evangelical tradition, and the

---

1. The core of this set of ideas emerged for me in a conversation with Jim Wallis in the early 1990s. As a magazine publisher he was attuned to these issues.

incarnational tradition.[2] What publishers discovered was that there were writers who were the preeminent voices in each of these fields. And those writers became the most sought after and the best-selling authors for publishers. For example, when a reader is looking for a book in the social justice field the names of Joan Chittister or Jim Wallis emerge over and over, or for the incarnational tradition the names Henri Nouwen or Joyce Rupp or Fredericka Matthews Green are unavoidable, or in the evangelical tradition the names of Hannah Whitehall Smith or Philip Yancey or Billy Graham or Max Lucado might pop up. And in the contemplative tradition most readers will recognize the names of Evelyn Underhill or Barbara Brown Taylor or Thomas Merton or Thomas Keating or Paula D'Arcy. But what I would bet money on is that most readers could not name the denominational affiliation of each of these writers. The shift is complete.

For many of these writers, and here is where Paula D'Arcy is an exemplar, their style and message goes beyond just crossing denominational lines to crossing religious lines and then even out into the broader world of people concerned about topics of human interest. Paula has accomplished that rare goal with this book.

---

2. Richard J Foster, *Streams of Living Water: Celebrating the Great Traditions of Christian Faith* (HarperSanFrancisco, 1998).

A Word from the Editor

Even more profound than that accomplishment is the rare but luminous authenticity that shines through this set of stories. All of us are hungry for this kind of writing and even more importantly for this kind of living. We want to know that Paula D'Arcy is a real person who actually lives the words she breathes out to us. I can tell you that she is that real person and that it gives me hope in all things spiritual, as it will you.

This book is a memoir, a slice of Paula's story that tells us about a particular issue. And it is in today's memoirs that most of us find and enjoy our stories of authentic spirituality. Several years ago a book agent friend told me that editors in New York were certain that the "memoir fad" was over and that she should not try to sell them any more memoirs. I laughed. People didn't want to read true personal stories any more? That was and is a ludicrous idea. And the "fad" is now as strong as ever and continues to be one of the staples of publishing. And this is especially true for those of us who live as close as we know how to that thin "veil" between ordinary life and spiritual life. Paula takes us there, and for a few moments we glimpse beyond the veil. You can trust her as your guide.

—*Roy M. Carlisle*
Senior Editor

Also by Paula D'Arcy

THE GIFT OF THE RED BIRD
A Spiritual Encounter

When Paula D'Arcy lost her husband and baby in a car crash, she began an inner search for a faith that was stronger than fear. In *Gift of the Red Bird* she shares her remarkable spiritual adventure: Paula literally journeyed alone into the wilderness for three days, allowing the Creator to speak through that creation. As she surrendered to the power of God alone, a red bird appeared and, without words, began to teach...

"To say that *The Gift of the Red Bird* moved me deeply seems inadequate. I wept for its beauty, pain, and joy. It is a powerful testimony to how the Divine woos the soul into a sacred embrace. Paula D'Arcy's vulnerability and courage in narrating her true story of this Divine encounter are remarkable." —Joyce Rupp

"It is all a matter of seeing, but we need seers to show us how. Paula D'Arcy shatters our poor sight and shows us light." —Richard Rohr

0-8245-1956-6, paperback

crossroad

Also by Paula D'Arcy

WHEN PEOPLE GRIEVE
The Power of Love in the Midst of Pain

Since the publication of her first bestseller, *Song for Sarah,* Paula D'Arcy has become an internationally renowned expert in grief and bereavement issues. Now in a completely revised and updated version of an earlier book, Paula helps us understand how to cope with the process of grief and also how to reach out to others in the pain of grief. This classic manual is full of practical advice.

Paula D'Arcy, author of the bestsellers *Gift of the Red Bird* and *Sacred Threshold,* is a former psychotherapist and president of the Red Bird Foundation. She is a frequent speaker in Europe and the United States and lives in northern California.

0-8245-2339-3, paperback

crossroad

Of Related Interest

Lyn Doucet and Robin Hebert
WHEN WOMEN PRAY
Our Personal Stories of Extraordinary Grace

"We are two ordinary women who, through God's grace, have had extraordinary experiences of prayer. In this book we share several of these experiences. We have no final answers about God, for in prayer we have experienced God as a beautiful dance of mystery. And yet we know that in the presence of this dance of love we have been transformed. And we now desire to invite you into this sacred dance of daily communion with God."

Includes original prayers and helpful tips for praying.

0-8245-2279-6, paperback

Check your local bookstore for availability.
To order directly from the publisher,
please call 1-800-707-0670 for Customer Service
or visit our Web site at *www.cpcbooks.com.*
For catalog orders,
please send your request to the address below.

THE CROSSROAD PUBLISHING COMPANY
16 Penn Plaza, Suite 1550
New York, NY 10001

All prices subject to change.

crossroad